PRAISE FOR THE AUTHOR

"He does for business what Nike does for sport."
RICHARD HYTNER, Deputy Chairman, Saatchi & Saatchi Worldwide

"A great combination of words and images that gets to the point fast
– and with distinctive style."
ROB GOFFEE, Emeritus Professor of Organizational Behaviour,
London Business School

"A treasure trove of laser-bright insights."
MARTY NEUMEIER, Author of Zag and The Brand Gap

"Wipe away the bullshit and liberate yourself to think more clearly,
act more effectively and get stuff done."
CHRIS HIRST, Global CEO, Creative, Author of No Bullshit Leadership

"Kevin has written a Tardis of a book. It packs an awful lot of ideas
and insights into a small and accessible package."
RICHARD SHOTTON, Author of The Choice Factory and The Illusion of Choice

"One thing remains constant with all of Kevin's books
– practical advice that makes us better."
RICHARD MORRIS, CEO, UK & Ireland, IPG Mediabrands

"These ways of working could prove contagious."
JONAH BERGER, Author of Contagious

PRAISE FOR
THE DIAGRAMS BOOK

"Here is a visual language that can be used to make one's case and win respect."
WILL HARRIS, Business Director, WPP

"I had been coveting a copy for a while, so I am dead chuffed
to actually get my hands on one."
RICHARD HUNTINGTON, Chairman & Chief Strategy Officer,
Saatchi & Saatchi

"I'm a big fan of visuals to help represent a point, so it really did the job."
MAT SEARS, Head of PR and Corporate Communications,
Everything Everywhere

"If I were to leave you with one last shape that represents my thoughts
on this book it would be ♥."
TRACY DE GROOSE, CEO, Dentsu Aegis Network UK

"Geometry turned into an engaging strategic toolkit.
This is a fun and richly rewarding read."
RICHARD SWAAB, Executive Vice Chairman AMV BBDO

"I love the simplicity of it all. Being a shape and visual person,
it is totally aligned with my kind of thinking. I can see some quick wins
using these ideas in workshops."
JUDY GOLDBERG, Executive Director, Leadership & Organization Development,
Sony Pictures Entertainment

DEDICATED TO CALISTA, THE QUEEN OF VISUAL THINKING.

Published by
LID Publishing
An imprint of LID Business Media Ltd.
LABS House, 15-19 Bloomsbury Way,
London, WC1A 2TH, UK

info@lidpublishing.com
www.lidpublishing.com

A member of:

businesspublishersroundtable.com

Printed by Imak Ofset

ISBN: 978-1-915951-03-8 (paperback)
ISBN: 978-1-915951-47-2 (hardback)
ISBN: 978-1-911687-57-3 (ebook)

Cover and page design: Caroline Li

THE
DIAGRAMS
BOOK

100 WAYS TO SOLVE ANY PROBLEM VISUALLY

KEVIN DUNCAN

MADRID | MEXICO CITY | LONDON
BUENOS AIRES | BOGOTA | SHANGHAI

FOR OTHER TITLES
IN THE SERIES ...

CONCISE
ADVICE
LAB

SMALL BOOKS: BIG IDEAS

CLEVER CONTENT, DYNAMIC IDEAS, PRACTICAL
SOLUTIONS AND ENGAGING VISUALS
A CATALYST TO INSPIRE NEW WAYS OF THINKING
AND PROBLEM SOLVING IN A COMPLEX WORLD

www.lidpublishing.com/product-category/concise-advice-series

CONTENTS

. . . .

PART FIVE: FLOWS & CONCEPTS

FOREWORD TO
ANNIVERSARY EDITION, 2024

I first made sense of the world through shapes.

In early learning, I discovered the star, circle, triangle and square and learned how to fit them into the correct holes on a board.

Then *Play School*, a favourite pre-school TV show, encouraged me to see how things were made by 'looking through the round, square or arched window,' depending on the day.

Words quickly took over. I was driven to learn more, use more, apply more, adding complexity and nuance. For me, more words meant progress.

Through that, I made a career in communications and words became 'my thing.' Again, I was rewarded for words and having a wide vocabulary. But maybe I'd also lost something along the way.

Recently I flicked through a shelf of my old hardback workbooks. They carried handwritten notes across decades of complex issues, actions and stories. They showed my thoughts, analysis, actions and attempts to make plans memorable.

And as I moved through the pages, the notes evolved.

There were two significant steps: a joined-up scrawl had switched to capital letters, and clear shapes and diagrams had emerged to help me to understand my thinking.

I had started to use fewer words with greater impact. Processes and flows were evident. My ideas were easier to read and recall. I could see the moment I'd been introduced to *The Diagrams Book* and started to apply its approach.

In an ever more complicated world, *The Diagrams Book* has helped me to visualise thoughts and simplify strategy – for myself, with colleagues and presenting to clients – and lived up to its promise to "solve any problem visually."

It has had a catalytic effect on the way I shape and present ideas. It has helped me to communicate insights, processes and actions, both visually and verbally, and to connect with audiences across cultures and mindsets. To give my thoughts shape.

Now, each time I have something tricky to process or distil, I dive into *The Diagrams Book* and find a solution. I can find stimulus, adopt or adapt a shape or flow, turn complexity into simplicity and find a memorable solution.

And as Kevin's *Cone of Learning* shows, we're three times more likely to remember what we have seen compared to what we have read.

Everyone will have their favourite diagrams; something that fits their way of thinking or their regular tasks. I love the Bow Tie, the Cultural Deadline, Three Buckets, Whittling Wedge, Barriers To Purchase Axis and the Loud Hailer.

You'll have your own and treasure different ones on different days for different projects.

Kevin's brilliant book has proved so valuable that I not only recommend it but regularly gift it. I'm sure you'll do the same. Recipients become better communicators, strategists or leaders, and evangelists themselves.

Looking at the testimonials *The Diagrams Book* has gathered over a decade - across industries, sectors and cultures - its applications are as wide as its influence. And translation into twenty languages is proof of how shapes can cut across continents and cultures.

Its genius is turning complexity into simplicity, in creating clarity and impact through ideas presented in shapes.

CHRIS HAYNES
Communications Consultant and Coach,
Former Director of Communications,
Sky Sports and England Cricket

FOREWORD TO
ORIGINAL EDITION, 2013

I am delighted Kevin has written this book. I love shapes as a way of expressing thoughts or ideas – it's the way my brain works. I think visually. Diagrams help to keep my thinking clear and simple, and I'm a big believer in keeping things simple.

With standing still no longer an option, we're all under pressure to get more done. Yet the world is more complicated and getting things done is more of a challenge. I regularly talk to clients about the 'how' being more of a challenge than the 'what.'

If we want to get more things done we need to simplify, and there lies the value of a good diagram – a simple visual representation of a strategy, thought or idea. We should embrace wholeheartedly any tools that help us to get things done, so this book is for anyone who wants to get stuff done.

People only remember 10% of what they read, but 30% of what they see. Shapes have an immediate advantage over words. And yet most businesses tend to focus on the written word. Don't get me wrong – I like words as much as the next person, but words can be, and often are, abused. There can be a temptation to write too much and that can make things complicated. Diagrams can be abused too, but not to the same degree. I believe thinking visually helps get to the simplicity of a thought.

I'm delighted Kevin has included all my favourite diagrams – circles, the classic pyramid, the funnel and the bow tie.

I started off my early marketing career using circles (great for target audiences), and the pie chart continues to be an easy way to understand sales breakdowns quickly. Concentric circles will always be useful, as the world doesn't always fit into neat and separate entities.

The pyramid immediately makes me think of Maslow's Hierarchy of Needs. I've used that many times to explain thoughts and ideas. As part of a team a few years ago, we used Maslow's Hierarchy to win a pitch for a big paint manufacturer – we explained how women saw colour and home design as a way of self-expression.

The bow tie is a good one. In its simplest form it represents lots of inputs, condensed into one simple expression or idea, then expressed back out into many different forms. It's really useful for marketers who need to use different data sources to develop an idea, and then activate that in many different ways.

Shapes and diagrams travel, and in a world where globalization is affecting many of us, that's important. Those of us in global businesses need our thinking to be able to work across borders, and there lies the value of visuals.

We are becoming a more visual society. More and more of us will be thinking visually in the years to come. We will all be embracing shapes and diagrams as a way of thinking.

If I were to leave you with one last shape that represents my thoughts on this book it would be ♥.

TRACY DE GROOSE
CEO, Dentsu Aegis Network UK

INTRODUCTION

Ten years ago I noticed that many of my attendees in training were taking notes in a new way – drawing shapes instead of old-fashioned longhand lecture notes.

So I wondered how many diagrams there were in my training materials. The answer was 46, so I added 4 more and wrote *The Diagrams Book*.

There is now an entire world market in visual thinking.

Having trained thousands of people, it is apparent that many find it hard to express ideas and solve problems purely with words.

Diagrams are superb for organizing your own thinking.

Once you have done that, you have a better chance of coming across as more strategic, or simply being better at explaining your point of view to colleagues and customers.

It is a delight to have the book coming back in a range of languages – from Japan, China and Korea, to Germany, Spain and Sweden.

Good luck, and keep me posted on the blog.

Kevin Duncan,
Westminster, 2024

PART ONE

TRIANGLES AND PYRAMIDS

A WORD ON
TRIANGLES
AND PYRAMIDS

The triangle is a design classic.

It captures the essence of any 1, 2, 3 or A, B, C sequence so beloved of people the world over.

Three blind mice. An Englishman, an Irishman and a Scotsman walk into a bar. *The Lord of the Rings* trilogy. Everybody loves things that come in threes.

So, if any three-pronged issue requires explanation, try a triangle.

But there's more.

Wedges can dramatize gradual increases or declines – building a story up, or narrowing options down.

Interlocking two triangles can show a mixture of both, or a transition from one state of affairs to another.

Pyramids can explain gradation and the components of a progression.

And, rather brilliantly, the space in the middle of a triangle offers a chance for a fourth component – most powerfully, the focal point of the issue in question.

1 **THE PYRAMID**

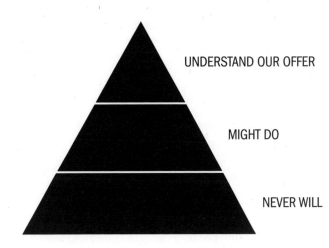

UNDERSTAND OUR OFFER

MIGHT DO

NEVER WILL

- The pyramid is one of the most versatile diagrams in the world.
- The base offers a platform, the middle a transition area, and the peak, (or capstone), an achievement, a destination or an elite group.
- It is very useful for categorizing discrete groups without overcomplicating matters.

- In this example, the top section represents people who understand a company's offer, the middle is people who might, and the base is people who never will. By populating the sections with prospect names or quantities, the viewer has an immediate grasp of what the new business strategy should be.
- Classically, high volume or mass market subjects will be at the base, with effort concentrating the higher one goes.
- The top usually represents a target or aspiration of some kind.
- The most rigorous versions are diligent enough to populate each layer with numbers, so that the size of the opportunity, or lack of it, is absolutely clear.

EXERCISE: *Choose an issue. Divide it into no fewer than three, and no more than five, stages, categories or segments. Put them in sequence. Choose a direction from top to bottom of the pyramid or vice versa. Add quantities to each layer if relevant.*

₂ THE SELLING PYRAMID

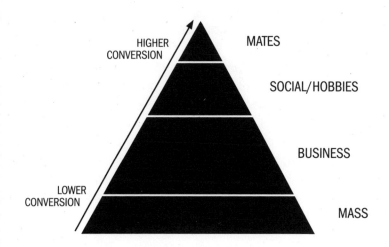

- Pyramids can be given multiple layers. For clarity, it is best not to have more than five layers, otherwise the information will become too cluttered.
- The selling pyramid is a good way to work out where to deploy your sales efforts.
- In this simple example, the size of the segment radiates downward from knowing a few close friends at the top, and then expanding in size via social and business contacts to arrive at a mass audience.

- Quantifying these sections helps someone who runs their own business to work out what to concentrate on, but is equally useful for large businesses.
- Direction and nature of opportunity can be added by including an arrow. In this case, the point being made is that the likelihood of converting to a sale will increase the more closely connected the potential purchaser is to the business owner.

EXERCISE: *Choose a product, brand or service you wish to sell. Use The Selling Pyramid to define who might buy it. Put them in sequence from a small to a large opportunity. Add quantities if possible for each layer, and then choose your easiest or most profitable segment as the place to start.*

THE CONE OF LEARNING

- The Cone of Learning was conceived by Edgar Dale in 1969.
- It uses the scale of the pyramid to make a number of points about how well (or poorly) we retain knowledge, in this case two weeks after being taught.
- The tiny tip of the pyramid is used to show that after this time we only remember 10% of what we read.
- This increases to 20% of what we hear, 30% of what we see, 50% of what we see *and* hear, and 70% of what we say.
- The large wide base is used to make the clinching point – that after two weeks we retain 90% of what we say *and* do.
- The space in the sections is used to give examples of what the nature of the learning techniques might be in each case.
- The system can be used for working out the right medium to use depending on the importance of the point you want to make, progressing from small at the top to large at the base.
- The moral is you can always increase your communication effectiveness by stepping up the medium you use. If you want your point to really stick then don't hide behind email. If you were going to send an email, then call. If you were going to call, then meet. If you can't meet, use modern technology to replicate those conditions, with a video call or webinar.

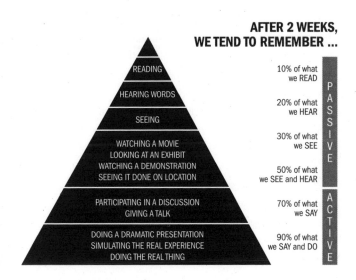

AFTER 2 WEEKS,
WE TEND TO REMEMBER ...

READING — 10% of what we READ

HEARING WORDS — 20% of what we HEAR

SEEING — 30% of what we SEE

WATCHING A MOVIE
LOOKING AT AN EXHIBIT
WATCHING A DEMONSTRATION
SEEING IT DONE ON LOCATION — 50% of what we SEE and HEAR

PARTICIPATING IN A DISCUSSION
GIVING A TALK — 70% of what we SAY

DOING A DRAMATIC PRESENTATION
SIMULATING THE REAL EXPERIENCE
DOING THE REAL THING — 90% of what we SAY and DO

PASSIVE

ACTIVE

EXERCISE: *Choose a point you really need to get across effectively. Use The Cone of Learning to set yourself a minimum target of 50% memory of your message after two weeks (see and hear), and work out the best way to achieve this. For a more ambitious version, set yourself a 90% target (say and do) to yield the optimum result.*

4 THE WHITTLING WEDGE

- The Whittling Wedge is brilliant for telling a strategic story and narrowing down options. This allows the presenter to explain their workings, show that a lot was considered, but still end with a clear, preferably single, recommendation.
- Starting on the left, many options can be introduced, analysed, and then systematically rejected, using as much rationale and detail as is appropriate to the subject.
- By the middle of the wedge, we should be down to a maximum of three or four possibilities.
- These can be analysed in even more detail, or even recommended for detailed research.
- Finally the presenter arrives on the right with a beautifully argued recommendation that has covered all considerations.
- Overall, whittling the argument in this way emulates how equation questions must be successfully answered in maths exams. You can't just stampede to the answer – you have to show your workings.
- The more complex the story, the more the audience appreciates this explanatory approach.

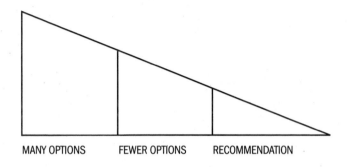

MANY OPTIONS FEWER OPTIONS RECOMMENDATION

EXERCISE: *Choose a presentation or story that needs explaining, ideally one with quite a few options or wide-ranging subject matter. Use The Whittling Wedge to start broad, and then reduce the number of options or topics systematically. Try to arrive at the end with one clear recommendation or point of view.*

5 **THE RISING WEDGE**

- The Rising Wedge is ideal for building a story, or demonstrating how something will develop over time.
- The steepness of the incline can be varied to indicate speed over a shorter time span.
- It can also be used as a partner to The Whittling Wedge, by expanding a story outward. For example, having whittled to the essence of a recommendation, the presenter can then explain how the idea can be used in many different formats, with multiple audiences, in different regions and so on.
- As with a pyramid, the recommended maximum number of subdivisions is five, in order to retain clarity.
- In this example, we examine the classic adoption sequence of a new product or craze. Early adopters are the first to get going, followed by the secondary and late adopters, followed at the end by the laggards.
- These sections are at their most powerful when populated by figures.
- Here we see that the majority of the market opportunity comes later, so a brand would be well advised to be patient.
- Data like these enable the presenter to tell a compelling strategic story, or explain where future effort should be expended in a convincing way.

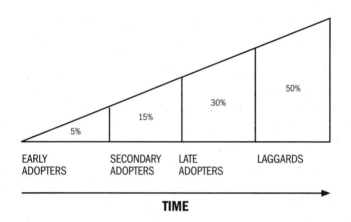

5%

15%

30%

50%

EARLY
ADOPTERS

SECONDARY
ADOPTERS

LATE
ADOPTERS

LAGGARDS

TIME

EXERCISE: *Choose a time period or point that needs expanding. Divide The Rising Wedge by time or segments. Add figures if relevant. Practise expanding the story from left to right.*

- The Interlocking Wedge allows two diametrically opposed approaches to be compared logically.
- The two extremes are placed to the far right and left, approaches A and B. At each extreme the approach taken would be 100% A or B.
- A manageable number of interlocking criteria are then chosen, in this case three: high (100% one approach), medium (60% one, 40% the other) and low (80:20).

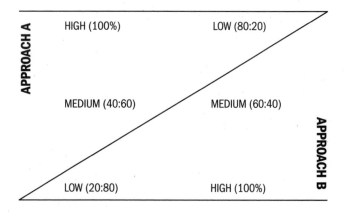

- By merging these criteria from left to right and vice versa, the diagram generates a series of possible permutations for resolving the issue.
- In this example there are six permutations, and each can then be analysed for suitability.

EXERCISE: *Choose an issue with two extremes. Place one at each end of The Interlocking Wedge. Choose a maximum of three permutations that deal with different ways in which the problem can be approached. Give the permutations a percentage ratio and place them above or below the diagonal as appropriate depending on severity. Review the different combinations and choose which will work best.*

- The IF Triangle is a crucial ally in any negotiation because it covers the only three variables that are ever at stake when a customer is considering whether to make a purchase.
- The three questions are always: Will it do the job? (quality) How much will it cost? (price) When can I have it? (timing)
- When negotiating, there can always be some flexibility on any two of these variables, but never on all three.

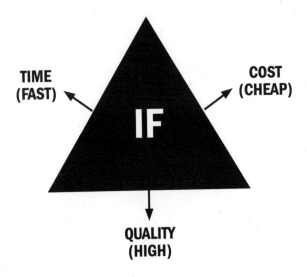

- For example, the price can usually be reduced if more time is allowed. Quicker delivery may be possible for a premium price. And although no one will ever admit to wanting low quality, things can often be short-circuited.
- It is called the IF Triangle because a good way to enact a successful negotiating stance is to start every sentence in the negotiation with the word *If*.
- It is impossible to finish a sentence that begins with *If* without attaching a condition – a crucial weapon in any successful negotiation.
- Examples include: *"If I have to deliver it by Friday, the price will have to increase,"* and *"If you need the price to reduce, I will need longer to do the job."*

EXERCISE: *Choose an issue that is the subject of negotiation. Write down the time, cost and quality parameters. Devise three sentences beginning with "If ..." that define your negotiation stance.*

THE F TRIANGLE

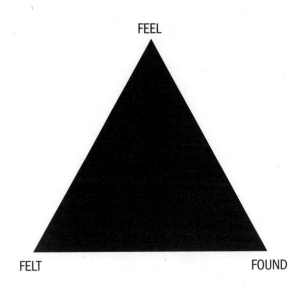

- The F Triangle is extremely helpful for overcoming objections to a sale.
- The three components are feel, felt and found.
- The idea is to compose a sentence that encourages a sceptical customer to reconsider their reservations and end up buying after all.

- The construction of the sentence will run along these lines: "I understand you *feel* x about subject y – I *felt* the same but once I discovered z I *found* it was more than worth the money."
- The personal 'I' can be replaced with the views of colleagues or other influencers, and the discovery element can be expressed as an experience, a product feature or an emotional benefit.

EXERCISE: *Choose a situation in which the potential customer doesn't want to buy from you or your company, or one in which they have significant doubts. Articulate how you feel about the subject, how others felt the same, and identify what they found to overcome their reservations and led to a sale. Now compose the sentence.*

9 THE BUSINESS
SATISFACTION TRIANGLE

- The Business Satisfaction Triangle deals with the three most important components that affect whether companies and their people find their work fulfilling.
- The three elements are fun (enjoyment), subject matter (intellectual interest and stimulation), and financial value (making a profit).
- If a business can tick all three criteria, then it has ideal work circumstances.
- It is important that a minimum of two of these criteria are met to make any project or customer relationship appealing.
- If only one can be ticked, then the business should seriously consider declining the work, or at the very least must change something significant.
- If none of the criteria apply, then the business should probably not proceed.

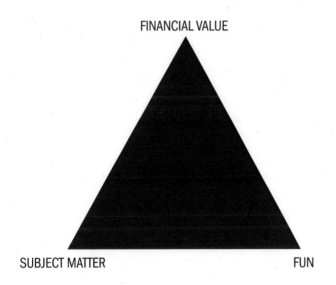

FINANCIAL VALUE

SUBJECT MATTER   FUN

EXERCISE: *Choose a client relationship, or a potential one. Use the three criteria to tick, score or predict their outcome. See how many criteria apply. Now decide whether to proceed with the relationship, or make important changes.*

THE PERSONAL MOTIVATION TRIANGLE

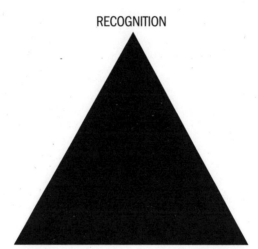

RECOGNITION

JOB SATISFACTION   FINANCIAL REWARD

- The Personal Motivation Triangle is ideal for use in appraisals when assessing morale and staff motivation in a member of staff or a team.
- It can also be used to assess your own personal circumstances.
- It maps out the three most important components that affect whether people find their work fulfilling.

- The three elements are recognition (status, progression and promotion), job satisfaction (intellectual interest and stimulation), and financial reward (salary and benefits).
- If an individual can tick all three, then they have the ideal work circumstances.
- If they are happy with two of these criteria then attention can be paid to improving the third.
- If only one can be ticked, then urgent and significant change is needed.
- If none apply, then either the employer should be acting urgently, or the individual should probably move job immediately if nothing can be changed.

EXERCISE: If you are conducting an appraisal, ask the person you are appraising to conduct the exercise, and examine the results to find out what matters to them the most. Use the findings as a basis for discussion or action. Design a graded scoring system if necessary. If you are doing it for yourself, take the three criteria and decide how happy you are with each of them. See how acute the problem is and then work out what needs to be changed.

11 THE FIVE DYSFUNCTIONS OF A TEAM PYRAMID

- According to Patrick Lencioni, five dysfunctions can ruin the effectiveness and cohesion of any team, particularly leadership teams.
- *Absence of trust.* This stems from an unwillingness to be vulnerable within the group. Those who are not open about mistakes and weaknesses make it impossible to build trust.
- *Fear of conflict.* Teams that lack trust are incapable of engaging in unfiltered debate.
- *Lack of commitment.* Without having aired their opinions openly, team members rarely buy in or commit to decisions, though they may feign it.
- *Avoidance of accountability.* Without committing to a clear plan of action, even the most focused people fail to call their peers on counterproductive actions and behaviour.
- *Inattention to results.* Failure to hold one another accountable creates an environment where team members put their individual or departmental needs above those of the team.

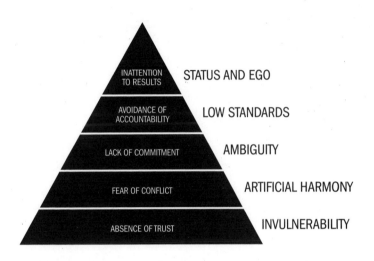

EXERCISE: *The model can be used effectively in any management team awayday. Discuss openly with the team how you can encourage the following: Trust (by overcoming invulnerability and admitting to weaknesses); Constructive conflict (to replace artificial harmony); Commitment (by removing ambiguity); Accountability (by raising low standards); and Inattention to results (by removing status and ego issues).*

12 THE BRIEFING STAR

- The Briefing Star was originally devised by this author in *The Ideas Book* in 2014 and has been used by thousands of people since.
- The best briefs are clinically simple. If you are running an ideas session, or simply setting yourself a task, you should restrict yourself to one sentence. This is worth spending a lot of time on, because if it is not clear, no decent response will be forthcoming.
- Start with what: What are we trying to achieve?
- Then confirm the sense of that by asking why: Why are we trying to do this?
- If the answers are too vague or unsatisfactory, then change the what, or scrap the project altogether.
- Then describe the who: Who is this aimed at?
- The brief can now be expressed as a statement *(Our objective is to revolutionize the X category)*, or a question *(How do we double the size of Brand X?)*.
- If the thinking is sufficiently clear and robust, it may be acceptable to have both an objective and a question: *Our objective is to revolutionize the X category. What single product feature would achieve this?*

EXERCISE: *Choose a business issue that needs serious attention. Spend time articulating it in as short and clear way as possible. First ask, what are we trying to achieve? Do not proceed until this is absolutely clear. If needed, ask the why question to cross check whether the what is sufficiently robust. Add the why. Experiment with using a statement as the brief, or a question, or both in tandem. Leave the result and come back to it later, make changes if necessary, then check with a respected colleague to see if they think it is a decent brief.*

WHY?

WHAT?

WHO?

THE RIGHT QUESTION

THE RIGHT STATEMENT

13 THE STARBURSTING TECHNIQUE

- Starbursting is a very close cousin of The Briefing Star.
- It is based on the six questions posed by Rudyard Kipling in his book *The Elephant's Child*:

    I keep six honest serving-men
    (They taught me all I know)
    Their names are What and Why and When
    And How and Where and Who
    I send them over land and sea
    I send them east and west
    But after they have worked for me
    I give them all a rest.

- This is not quite as irritating as a child constantly asking why until you are driven to distraction, but it performs a similar role. The idea is that so-called 'silly' questions can often flush out important issues that are being overlooked and alert the proposer of an idea to the fact that they may need to investigate much deeper than they currently have.
- Each word in the six-pointed star can be used as the starter word for a longer question, such as 'How are we going to finance this idea?'

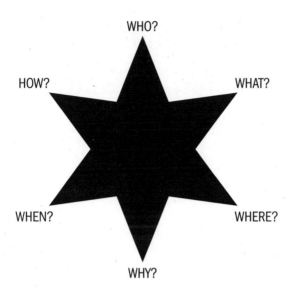

WHO?

HOW?   WHAT?

WHEN?   WHERE?

WHY?

- Generate as many as possible to start with but do not answer
  them. Sometimes the sheer volume of questions shows that the
  idea cannot survive under the weight of the scrutiny – in which
  case, the star will have burst. If there are just a few, then answer
  them comprehensively to see whether it is advisable to proceed.

EXERCISE: *Take a project that is important and likely to take up
a lot of time and resources. Subject it to the six questions. Keep
repeating them until everyone has run out of questions. If the
volume is large and it is clear that there are too many that cannot
be resolved, then consider ditching the project. If there are just
a few, then spend time working out the answers. If they can be
answered satisfactorily, consider proceeding.*

14

THE TRUST AND COOPERATION WEDGE

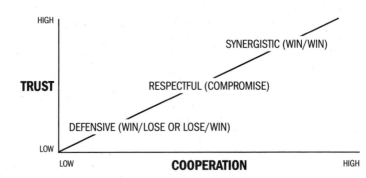

- Wedges are a good way of demonstrating how two elements can work well together, and what happens if they are not present.
- This example comes from the classic book *The 7 Habits of Highly Effective People* by Stephen Covey.
- Trust and cooperation are mapped against each other from low to high.
- Where both are low, people are suspicious and defensive. This either means that someone wins and someone loses, or there could even be complete deadlock.

- At the middle level, reasonable levels of both are more likely to lead to a respectful exchange of views, and ideally a sensible compromise based on different views that all contribute to a stronger outcome.
- Where trust and cooperation are both high, full synergy is achieved, often described as a win/win. Covey described this as an attitude of needing to understand the other person's perspective because of an innate belief that they are intelligent, competent and committed.

EXERCISE: Choose a board, team or committee in your business. Plot their degrees of trust and cooperation from defensive to respectful to synergistic. If they are the latter, you are unlikely to have issues. If both trust and cooperation are low, you need to work out why and come up with ideas to improve them. Use this to improve communication levels in any group.

15

THE PYRAMID DIAMOND TRANSFORMATION

THE CHANGING SHAPE OF BRITAIN

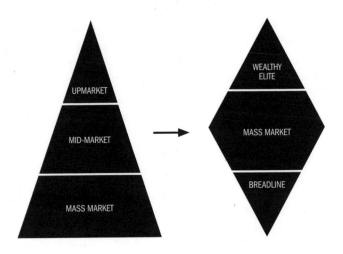

- This elegant pair of diagrams was revealed in a presentation by the then-called Trinity Mirror publishing house, owners of, among others, *The Daily Mirror* newspaper.

- The pyramid on the left represents the stratified layers of class distinction in Britain up until the turn of the century, with upmarket and mid-market being 'underpinned' by the mass market.
- As affluence increased in the 2000s, the shape changed significantly, with some slipping below the breadline, a wealthy elite becoming more and more so, and with the mass market expanding – essentially coming to regard private homes, cars, regular holidays and so on as the norm.
- A change of shape can be a dramatic way to encapsulate a change of state, without the need for multiple charts or many words.
- Note the use of the arrow to show the Transformation.

EXERCISE: Consider any situation in which there has been a fundamental change in circumstance. Select a shape for the original state of affairs, and a different one for the new state. If necessary, divide the shape into elements to add detail. As a sense check, show someone each shape separately to make sure they are indeed representative of what they are trying to convey. Then show them the pair to see if it conveys the point you want to make.

16

THE INVERTED LEADERSHIP PYRAMID

- The Inverted Leadership Pyramid is from Chris Hirst's excellent book, *No Bullsh*t Leadership*. (He didn't give the diagram that title, this author did).
- On the left is the old-fashioned, traditional way of running a company, with leadership behaviour characterized by telling everyone below them what to do. Each of the 10 downward arrows represents members of staff slavishly carrying out instructions from the top when interacting with their customers. This creates dependent cultures where talented people are often discouraged from thinking and acting for themselves.
- On the right is the modern, preferable approach, in which leaders ask how they can help support staff in their interactions with customers
- If you are a leader wishing to unlock your team's maximum potential, then you need to build a culture where everybody is focused on solving the challenges they face. That means making the people on the frontline the most important organizational figures. It transforms the leader into a mentor or coach, adding humility and facilitation.
- As with The Pyramid Diamond Transformation, note the use of the arrow to show the transition.

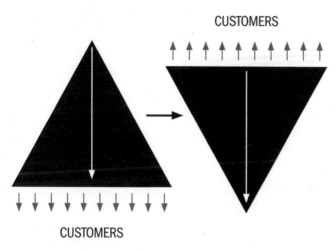

CUSTOMERS

CUSTOMERS

Leadership behaviour characterized
by telling those below them what
to do

Leadership behaviour characterized
by asking
"How can I help?"

EXERCISE: *Consider the shape and structure of a company, department, unit or team. Experiment with some shapes to demonstrate how it currently works. Consider if this is a good shape, or if it needs to transform into something else, and find a better shape. Place the old one on the left and the desired new one on the right. Test this on a colleague to see if it conveys what you want.*

17

THE ISHIKAWA FISHBONE DIAGRAM

- Dr Kaoru Ishikawa developed this type of diagram at the University of Tokyo in the 1940s. It was initially designed as a product improvement tool but has since taken on something of a life of its own as a general problem-solving device. Its principal purpose is to help understand the many causes that may contribute to a particular result.

- Such a diagram helps you to see every possible cause leading or contributing to a particular result. It is closely related to the Japanese belief that quality improvement should be a continual process, and that customer service is as important as high-quality products.

- It works well when thinking has fallen into the same old patterns, or where there is a need to reveal new connections or links that have not been obvious so far.

- The wording in this particular example is taken from *The Smart Solution Book* by David Cotton, and deals with the problem of too few clients, and what all the possible causes might be.

- A simplified alternative is on the next page.

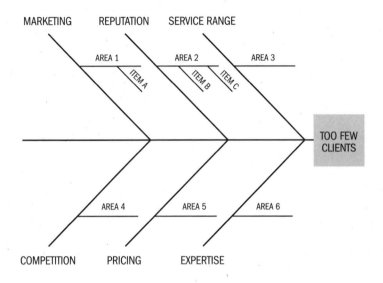

EXERCISE: Identify something that needs careful analysis – probably something that is not working well in your business. Draw the main spine of the 'fish,' and then start adding 'ribs' that may be causing the difficulty. Keep going until the fishbone is comprehensive. Then look at each element and define all related reasons until the diagram is complete. Find remedies based on the analysis.

18 THE SOLUTION
EFFECT ANALYSIS

- This is essentially an application of a standard fishbone diagram.
- It is the reverse of a cause-and-effect diagram and is designed to check if a solution does actually solve a problem. This offers a failsafe before implementing something that may have unexpected and undesirable consequences.
- The 'trunk and branch' design in a triangular rendition enables you to distinguish between the major and minor effects that the proposed solution might have. The major ones are placed in a box, and the minor ones expressed as offshoots or branches from there.
- The process requires an open mind, an honest attitude and a good working knowledge of a company, category or product.
- With this approach, pitfalls or entire failures should be identified before they have become reality.

EXERCISE: *Think of a problem that needs solving and settle on an agreed working solution. Gather colleagues who have the right spirit of open mindedness, honesty and knowledge of the issue. Outline the solution and predict the major effects it may have. Then dig deeper to anticipate the minor effects. See if the process unearths something unexpected that needs to be amended or rethought.*

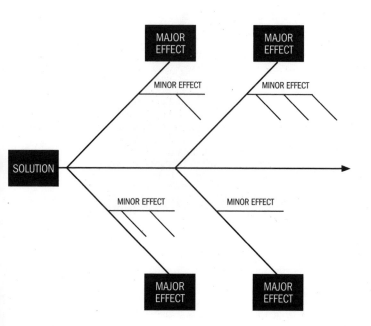

THE CONVINCE ME PYRAMID

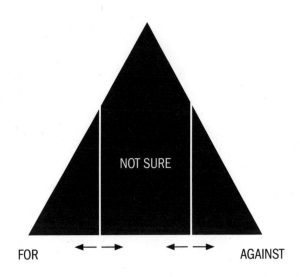

NOT SURE

FOR ←→ ←→ AGAINST

- The Convince Me Pyramid is a decision-making tool that allows you to work out whether to proceed with something or not. It is most useful when working with teams but can also be used by an individual with mixed feelings on a decision or proposed direction.
- The total area of the pyramid represents the full range of opinions from those who are for the idea, through those who are not sure, to those against it.

- Ask yourself or the team who is for the idea. Plot the vertical line to denote the weight of opinion in favour. Then repeat for those against. If there are abstainers or uncertain participants, represent their uncertainty with a middle ground zone of 'not sure.'
- After discussing what would make more people vote for the idea, try again and see if opinion has moved in a favourable direction. If it hasn't, accept that there is too much resistance and think of a better idea.
- If a team is physically present in the same room, this technique can be enacted physically, with team members voting by moving across the room toward 'for' or 'against' to show collective weight of opinion.
- The entire pyramid can be redrafted with different language such as acceptance on the left, resistance on the right, and indifference in the middle, *ad infinitum*.

EXERCISE: *Select a topic or project that requires a decision. If working on your own, plot your opinion on the pyramid. If working with a team, represent their views in the same way. Discuss reservations and see if they can be overcome. If they can, proceed. If they cannot, accept the rejection of the concept and work on something better.*

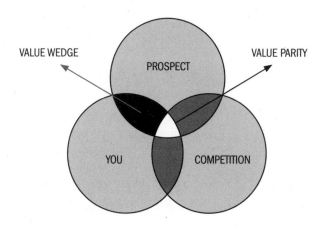

- The Value Wedge is a concept developed in a book called *Conversations That Win the Complex Sale* by Peterson & Riesterer. The diagram above shows its origin. It starts with a three-way Venn diagram mapping you (your offer) against the competition and your prospect(ive) customer. The Value Wedge lies at the intersection of you and your prospect, and needs to be defensible against value parity with the competition, where everything is par and you have no advantage.

- The resulting wedge shown on the right has three important components: it is unique to you, it is important to your prospect, and it is defensible against the competition. Should this be true of your product or service on all fronts, you are in what the authors call a Power Position.

POWER POSITION

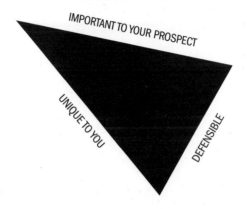

IMPORTANT TO YOUR PROSPECT

UNIQUE TO YOU

DEFENSIBLE

- This technique provides a valuable three-way perspective through which to assess whether you do indeed have the right components to enable you to secure a new customer.

EXERCISE: Choose a product or service that you believe could be a sales success. Start with a three-way Venn diagram plotting you, your prospect and the competition. Extract the Value Wedge and scrutinize its elements. Is what you have to offer important to your prospect? Is it unique to you? Is it defensible against value parity in relation to your competition? If the answer is no to all three, you are onto a loser. If the answer is yes to all three, you are onto a winner. Anything in between needs further analysis.

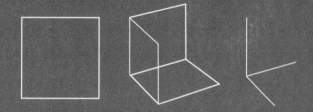

PART TWO

SQUARES AND AXES

A WORD ON
SQUARES
AND AXES
· · · · · · · · · · · · · · · · · · ·

There's nothing square about squares.

One straight line can express time or direction.

Two can provide horizontal and vertical axes.

Make them cross and you have a grid.

Add more and you have a square.

Grids generate quadrants and are great for separating elements and mapping markets.

Two axes with different attributes can be overlaid, and the exercise can be repeated many times until clarity is revealed.

Culture plays a part in which quadrant is viewed as the most desirable – top right is favoured in most of the Western world, whereas Arab countries read right to left.

Scale can be adjusted to dramatize the size of the problem or opportunity.

GOOD

CONFIRM RELEVANCE AND KEEP	REAFFIRM RELEVANCE AND USE TO INSPIRE MORE
GET RID OF IMMEDIATELY	ANALYSE WHY, LEARN LESSONS AND DESIGN NEW ONES

OLD ← → NEW

BAD

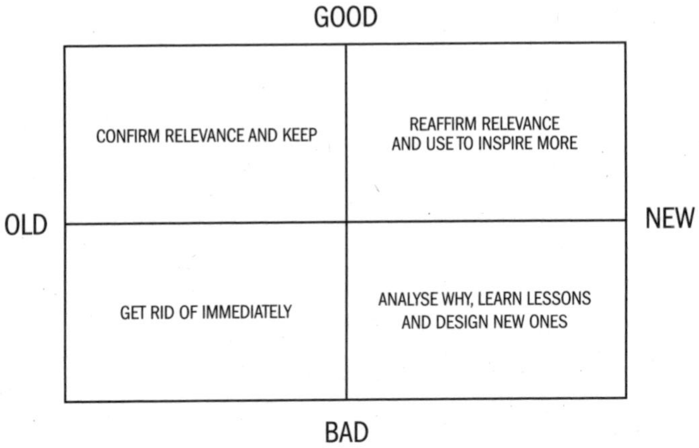

- This diagram helps to disentangle the good and bad elements of your working life, the business practices of a company, or even your personal habits.
- The vertical axis represents good at the top, and bad at the bottom.
- The horizontal axis represents old on the left, and new on the right.
- The pane allows you to categorize processes, techniques or habits. If something is old and good, then it goes in the top left quadrant and so on.

- If you have several practices in the 'good and old' segment, then that is fine. They have obviously stood the test of time, and do the job.
- If you have several of them in the 'good and new' section, even better. This means you are generating new ideas that really work. A blend of old and new is healthy.
- If there is anything in the 'new and bad' area, it needs careful analysis. It takes guts to reject an idea or process that has only recently been introduced, but surgery here is almost certainly necessary.
- Anything in the 'old and bad' quadrant is clearly not working and should be dropped immediately.

EXERCISE: Choose a subject to analyse. Select a manageable number of items to review – no more than 10 or 12. Work through them allocating each one to the relevant quadrant. Write an action list based on what needs to be done as a result.

URGENT

DELEGATE
OR DO FIRST, QUICKLY

DO NOW

NOT
IMPORTANT

IMPORTANT

IGNORE OR CANCEL

THINK AND PLAN

NOT URGENT

- The Priority Matrix helps establish what order of priority you are going to give to the jobs on your checklist.
- It can equally be applied to a day, a week, a month or even a year.
- The vertical axis represents urgent/not urgent, and the horizontal one is important/not important.
- If it is urgent and important, it falls in the top right, and you should do it now. The precise definition of 'now' may vary. Start with today and put the tasks in priority order.

- If it is urgent but not important, delegate it if you can, or do it quickly first to get it out of the way and meet the deadline.
- If it is important but not urgent, think about what you need to do and plan when you are going to do it. Be sure to put this planned time into your diary immediately – do not delay it and thus create yet another task.
- If it is neither important nor urgent, then you should question why you are doing it at all. If possible, ignore or cancel these tasks.

EXERCISE: *Take your list of things to do. Choose a helpful time period, such as a day, week or month. Draw the diagram and place each task in the appropriate quadrant. Methodically work through the action, starting with the most urgent.*

- The Market Map is a highly effective and very flexible way to establish clarity and strategic authority when looking at any market.
- Start by selecting two important factors in the market in question. For example, in the automotive market these might be price and safety reputation.
- Plot two overlapping axes from high to low, always placing the high ends to the top and right.
- Place your company and any competitors on the grid. So in this example a car with a good safety reputation and a high price would appear top right.
- Use the results to identify gaps in the market, or significant overlaps. Being out on your own could either be good (more distinctive) or bad (what do the others know that you don't?).
- If presenting to win a pitch, pointing out some current deficiencies and explaining how your proposals will improve matters (moving toward the top right) can be very powerful.
- The arrow from the central box pointing top right indicates your intended direction of travel. Most strategies are designed to respond to a need, so this suggests the beneficial trajectory that will occur if your proposal is accepted.

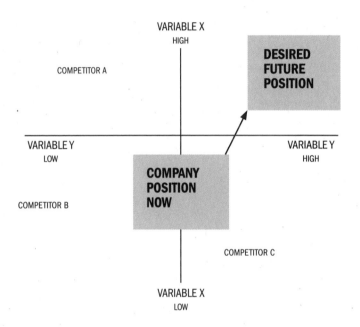

VARIABLE X
HIGH

COMPETITOR A

DESIRED
FUTURE
POSITION

VARIABLE Y
LOW

VARIABLE Y
HIGH

COMPANY
POSITION
NOW

COMPETITOR B

COMPETITOR C

VARIABLE X
LOW

EXERCISE: *Choose a market or category to look at. Choose your first two variables. Place your company or brand, and your competitors, on the grid. Repeat as often as desired with different variables and new combinations. Examine the results, decide where the best opportunities are and what the next appropriate action is.*

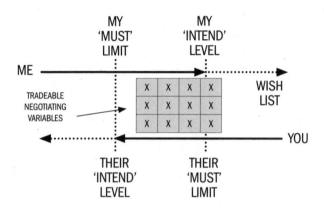

- The Bargaining Arena is excellent for preparing for a negotiation.
- View yourself or your company as being on the left of the diagram, with the other person or company approaching the issue from the right.
- The first point on the negotiation line is your 'must' limit – the limit below which you simply cannot go. So, for example, if it is a financial negotiation and you are selling on a product or service that you have bought in for £7,000, then £7,000 is your bare minimum.

- The next point is your 'intend' level – the amount you intend to get. In this example this might be £9,000 to allow a sensible margin on the transaction.
- Your wish list area includes any other benefits you would wish to have if the negotiation is going particularly well.
- Plotting the other negotiator's likely 'must', 'intend' and wish list points creates an overlap area in the centre.
- This is The Bargaining Arena, where a series of tradeable negotiating variables can be identified and used to bargain with. Trading these will allow both parties to come away satisfied.

EXERCISE: *Choose a negotiation topic. Work out your minimum 'must' limit. Now add your 'intend' level. Think of a wish list to add if you succeed in achieving your 'must' and 'intend' early. Repeat the exercise imagining you are the other party. Look at the overlapping needs and conclude what you believe to be the most important negotiating variables. Now plan your negotiating approach.*

25 THE BRAVERY SCALE

```
0 |_____|_____|_____| 10
  CONSERVATIVE              AVERAGE     BRAVE
```

- The Bravery Scale is a good way to establish how adventurous projects or proposals should be before a lot of time and effort is spent preparing them.
- In a healthy and open relationship with a customer, they should be asked: "How brave would you like our proposal to be?"
- A score out of 10 is generated to see whether conservative (below 5), average (5-7), or brave (above 7) levels are desired.
- The project leader or proposal writer can then consider:
  1. How adventurous is the company culture?
  2. How adventurous is the individual?
  3. Is there a difference between the two?
  4. Bearing all this in mind, how brave should our targets be?
- The scores can be blended to create one overall figure. For example, a conservative company asking for brave work may need to have its scale weighted downward to reflect their overall conservatism.

- The questions can of course be varied to suit the nature of the work.
- When the work is reaching conclusion, the scale helps to remind all present what level of bravery was requested in the first place, and provides a measure with which to compare.
- The scale is particularly useful to both sides in a service relationship such as a client and agency, where the bravery of work is frequently under discussion.

EXERCISE: *Choose a client or a proposal. Consider what questions would provide the most helpful guide. Ask the person or team who will be receiving the proposal to answer them. Use the responses to inform colleagues who are working on the proposal what is expected. Judge the ideas against the scale before deciding which to present and use the scale to frame expectations when presenting.*

TO PURCHASE AXIS

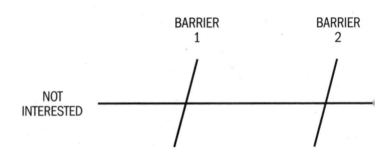

BARRIER 1

BARRIER 2

NOT INTERESTED

- Lines and axes can be helpful to demonstrate a progression from one state of affairs to another.
- In the Barriers to Purchase Axis, inactivity or disinterest is shown on the left, and interest or action on the right.
- Each notch of the axis represents a barrier to action, in this case a series of reasons why the potential customer will not purchase a product.
- By mapping the decision-making process diagrammatically, each barrier to purchase can be identified and isolated.
- Put yourself in the position of the customer, and assume they will reject your proposal. What will their objections be? These are the barriers.

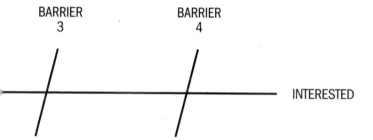

BARRIER
3

BARRIER
4

INTERESTED

- A plan to knock each one down can then be devised.
- Consider that if there are several barriers, it may take time to knock them all down, especially if your evidence is detailed. Avoid rushing and, in particular, allow the customer time to come round to your way of thinking without losing face.

EXERCISE: *Choose a product and a potential customer type. Use the axis to plot all the reasons stopping someone from purchasing. If relevant, put the barriers to purchase in chronological order, or place the biggest or hardest ones first, to the far left. Then come up with a plan to knock down each barrier.*

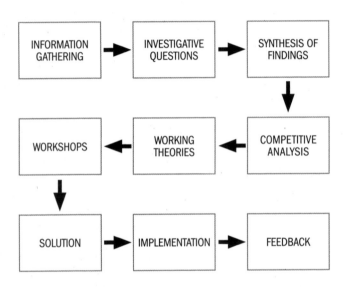

- The Box Process enables any work system to be explained simply.
- Each box contains a stage of work to be done. The descriptions inside them should be short and clear, and durations can be added to each if helpful.
- Each stage is linked by a directional arrow that shows what happens next, and it is important that the sequence is accurate.
- In this example there are nine stages, moving from information gathering through working theories to implementation and feedback.

- A cost per stage can be added to each box to help clarify the value of each.
- A process needs to have a minimum of three stages to make the chart worthwhile; one with over nine stages is likely to be too complex.

EXERCISE: *Take a process and break it down into stages. Place each stage in a box, make sure the sequence is correct, and link them with arrows. Make the descriptions as simple as possible. Add durations and costs per stage if helpful. Test-drive on a colleague to make sure all is clear.*

- The Long Tail was described by Chris Anderson in the book of the same name in 2006.
- The received wisdom in most markets is that high volume 'hits' are the best way to make money, as in a million-selling album.
- Anderson's Long Tail theory pointed out that the arrival of the internet had removed the need for much of the infrastructure required to generate and support a hit, such as costly premises, storage facilities, distribution, packaging, labour and so on.
- Instead, a 'long tail' of many niche products selling at modest volumes can actually add up to more sales in total than the one-off hit.
- Overall, use of The Long Tail diagram helps to identify the pros and cons of a high volume hit versus a series of smaller volume niches requiring far less investment and resources.

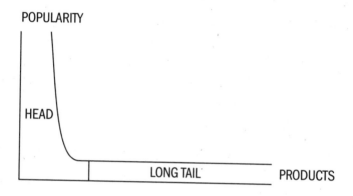

EXERCISE: Choose a market and identify what product and volume represents a hit. Plot this on The Long Tail diagram. Then identify a set of products that are niche, but which can be made available with minimal associated costs such as distribution and so on. Quantify each extreme to guide where the true market opportunity lies.

- A simple classic, the histogram uses stacked oblongs to represent volume, value, percentage, or any other quantities that require comparison.
- Traditionally, the highest value is placed on the left, with the remainder ranked in descending order to the right.
- The left hand vertical axis should be given a clear and accurate scale.
- If all the data is a snapshot of one moment in time, then the horizontal axis can be left unlabelled.
- Histograms can also be used to show data over time, with each block denoting a time period such as a day, week, month or year.
- If you are drawing a time-based histogram, then the units of time need to be clearly labelled on the horizontal axis, as in Jan, Feb, Mar, etc.

AMOUNT

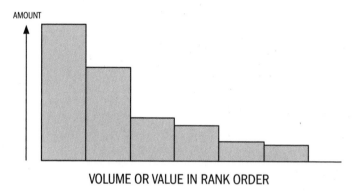

VOLUME OR VALUE IN RANK ORDER

EXERCISE: *Choose a data set that currently only exists in numerical format. Decide whether you want a snapshot of a moment in time, or a view over time. Convert the numbers into proportional blocks to generate the histogram. The visual representation of the data may well reveal more than just staring at a set of numbers.*

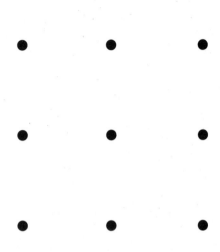

- We finish this part with a fun diagram that has infuriated people for years.
- In the Gottschaldt Figurine, or nine-dot game, there are three rows of three dots, forming what looks like a box or square.
- The precise origin of the game is the source of some debate, but management thinker John Adair claims to have introduced the idea himself in 1969.

- The challenge is to join all the dots without taking your pen off the paper, using no more than four straight lines.
- There are various ways to solve it, and two possible solutions are on the next page – don't look yet if you can resist it.
- The point is that, if you think of the dots as a box, you can't solve it.
- That is why the game is the origin of the phrase *thinking outside the box*.
- However, contrary to what this piece of jargon suggests, most studies show that problems are more likely to be solved when subject to quite tight constraints, so in reality it pays to think *inside* the box.

EXERCISE: *Before looking at the next page, draw nine dots on a blank page as it appears in the diagram. Now try to join all the dots using no more than four lines, and without taking the pen off the paper.*

GOTTSCHALDT FIGURINE SOLUTIONS

SOLUTION Nº 1

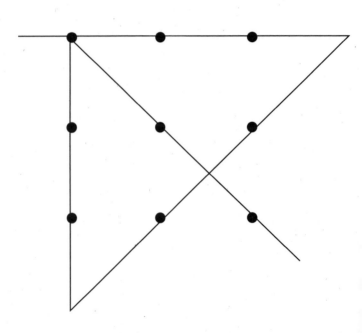

SOLUTION Nº 2

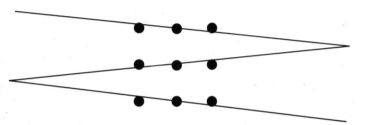

31

THE WIN/WIN MATRIX
. . . .

- This is a classic from Stephen Covey – the Win/Win matrix. This plots consideration on the vertical axis from low to high, and courage on the horizontal from low to high. Consideration means paying attention to the other person or party, and not being selfish. Courage means being brave and not being pushed around.
- Where both consideration and courage are low, everybody loses. This is usually down to both parties being too selfish or stubborn to adjust their attitude or position.
- In a win/lose position, the winner feels triumphant but may have ruined the chance of any long-term relationship by riding roughshod over the loser.
- In a lose/win position, the loser has allowed themselves to be pushed around through lack of courage.
- So win/win is where you want to be, with both parties feeling that they have achieved something positive and helpful from the transaction. This is described as an abundance mentality, where people agree that there is something for everyone in the deal.

EXERCISE: Consider a deal or negotiation that you are facing. Draw up the matrix as described. Insert the relevant variables into the correct quadrant. Eliminate flaws and move to the top right if possible, defining what would constitute a win/win for both parties.

32

THE TIME
MANAGEMENT MATRIX

	URGENT	NOT URGENT
IMPORTANT	Crises Pressing problems Deadline-driven projects	Prevention, PC activities Relationship building Recognizing new opportunities Planning, recreation
NOT IMPORTANT	Interruptions, some calls Some email, some reports Some meetings Proximate, pressing matters Popular activities	Trivia, busy work Some email Some phone calls Time wasters Pleasant activities

- The Time Management Matrix by Steven Covey can be viewed alongside The Priority Matrix to provide more detail and examples.
- The important/not and urgent/not criteria remain the same but appear in a different orientation, still generating four quadrants, but in different places.
- Urgent/important activities appear top left, and include crises, pressing problems and deadline-driven projects. This is all a form of 'production.'
- Important/not urgent activities include prevention, production capabilities (PC) activities, relationship building, recognizing new opportunities, planning and recreation.
- Urgent/not important activities include interruptions, some calls, (e)mail, reports, meetings and so on.
- Most of the activities in the bottom right quadrant are a waste of time.
- Update this matrix on your own terms to reflect modern technology and other circumstances.

EXERCISE: *Take your list of stuff to do, or an entire status report of jobs, and drop each one into one of the four quadrants. Then organize your working day/week/month accordingly.*

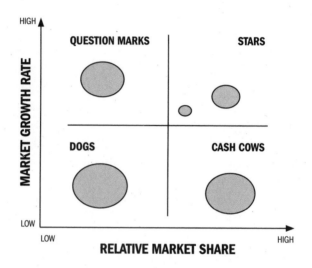

- The Boston Matrix was invented by the Boston Consulting Group and can be used to analyse a portfolio of products and establish what to do with them. It classifies them by relative market share (does the product or service have high or low market share?) and market growth rate (are the number of potential customers growing or not?).

- There are various versions of it, and sometimes the boxes are shown in different places, but the elements are the same. Products with high growth and market share are called stars, high share with low growth are cash cows, low on both are described as dogs, and high growth/low share are question marks to be monitored.
- This brutal but simple technique enables businesses to make clear decisions about whether to support or withdraw their products. Dogs are usually removed, cash cows allowed to continue, stars backed heavily, and question marks approached with a 'wait and see' brief.

EXERCISE: *Take a portfolio of products or services and put each one in a quadrant. Or apply the same approach to the projects you are working on. Use the findings to decide where to increase or decrease time and resources on products.*

	GENERAL	CONCRETE
INSPIRATIONAL	VISION/MISSION	ESSENTIAL INTENT Makes one decision that eliminates 1,000 later decisions
BLAND	VALUES	QUARTERLY OBJECTIVE

- This helpful grid features in a book called *Essentialism* by Greg McKeown. It helps companies to work out what they are all about. Instead of having axes with a range, it distinguishes on the vertical axis between bland and inspirational (but not on a spectrum), and between general and concrete on the horizontal. In this context, concrete means something tangible with a clear proof point, such as an absolute number of sales.

- Bottom left, values are usually bland and rarely concrete. They are broadly useful but often too vague to give specific guidance about direction.
- Bottom right, quarterly objectives are certainly concrete but rarely inspirational.
- Top left, a vision or mission can certainly be inspirational, but not immediately concrete. As such, it remains hard to pin down and/or prove that progress is genuinely happening.
- Top right, an *essential intent* needs to be both inspirational and concrete. That means it has true meaning and is measurable, such as "To get everyone in the country online by year X." This degree of clarity can eliminate thousands of later decisions.

EXERCISE: *Draw together elements from your company's vision, values, mission, objectives and so on. Place them in the grid based on their degree of blandness or inspirational qualities and general or concrete qualities. Try to generate an essential intent that is both inspirational and concrete.*

	KNOWN TO SELF	NOT KNOWN TO SELF
KNOWN TO OTHERS	OPEN AREA OR ARENA	BLIND SPOT
NOT KNOWN TO OTHERS	HIDDEN AREA OR FAÇADE	UNKNOWN

- The Johari Window is designed to improve self-awareness and personal development among individuals when they are in a group. It was invented by American psychologists Joseph Luft and Harry Ingham in 1955. The name 'Johari' came from joining their first two names.

- Top left, in the open area or arena the information about the person (attitudes, behaviour, emotions, feelings, skills, views, etc.) is known by the person as well as by others in the group.
- In the blind spot top right, the individual is unaware of information about themself but the others in the group are aware of it.
- Bottom left represents information that is known to the individual but kept unknown from others - often personal information which they feel reluctant to reveal.
- In the unknown area, no one knows the information.
- Information migrates across the four quadrants through honesty, self-realization and open communication.

EXAMPLE: *This technique requires a healthy dose of honesty from all team members because they will have to reveal things about themselves and discover other peoples' views of them. Do not proceed if this is too uncomfortable. With a high trust team, most participants should be able to exchange information to increase understanding and remove blind spots.*

HAPPINESS GRID

- The Conditional Happiness Grid deals with states of mind. The vertical axis maps knowledge in the broadest sense – self-awareness, learning about the world in general and experience.

- The horizontal axis represents a spectrum from pessimism to optimism.

- Those who are pessimistic and have low knowledge (everything from self-awareness to possibilities that can improve their circumstances and frame of mind) may well fall into desperation.

- Those who combine (albeit unintentionally) pessimism with high knowledge and awareness may well escalate issues so that they suffer from anxiety.

- Optimists with low knowledge (a restricted worldview) are likely to exist in a state of unconditional happiness – not necessarily a bad thing.

- Those with high knowledge (a broad worldview) and an optimistic outlook will most likely have conditional happiness - a positive but realistic outlook that has the power to allow the individual to keep everything in context.

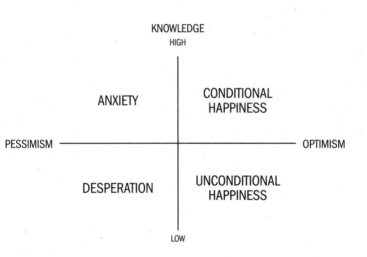

EXERCISE: Use the grid first to score yourself on the optimist/pessimist axis. Then apply your knowledge rating. Consider any action that might move you to a better place. Then give yourself a score for optimism and do the same. The technique can also be applied to partners, colleagues and other interested parties to improve self-awareness and work through issues.

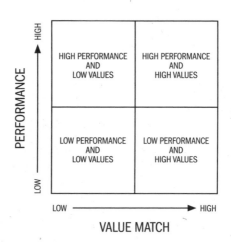

- This grid was generated by Jack Welch when he was CEO of the biggest company in the world at the time, General Electric. He was a highly controversial figure whose methods many regarded as questionable. Nevertheless, it attempts to deal with staff issues that always occur in companies, and can still be scrutinized in a modern context – that is to say: performance and values.
- Starting at the tough end of things, bottom left, if an individual's performance is low and so is the (lack of) match between their values and those of the company, then they should leave (or be forced to).

- Top right requires little explanation – this individual is spot on for fit and achievement.
- Anyone in the bottom right quadrant requires coaching to help them improve their performance.
- The really tricky one is top left – they are delivering but they are not tonally right for the company. These characters usually achieve their ends by breaking all the rules and marginalizing their colleagues.

EXERCISE: *Choose a team to look at. Consider each individual and place them in one of the four quadrants. See what level of consensus you have with your team about who sits where. Look at the proportion of each type of person. Do you have significant issues to deal with? If time allows, apply the technique to the entire company.*

38 THE RADICAL
CANDOR MATRIX

CARE PERSONALLY

RUINOUS EMPATHY

RADICAL CANDOR

DON'T CHALLENGE

CHALLENGE DIRECTLY

MANIPULATIVE INSINCERITY

OBNOXIOUS AGGRESSION

DON'T CARE

- The Radical Candor Matrix was first introduced in 2017 by Kim Scott in her book *Radical Candor*.
- Radical Candor means that bosses have to care personally and challenge directly, and according to the author, it only works properly if you do both.
- As you can see from the matrix, challenging directly without caring personally is just obnoxious aggression, and that's not helpful to anyone.

- Caring personally without challenging people on their deficiencies is arguably almost as bad because it creates ruinous empathy, in which the individual is allowed to stumble along with no feedback in a seemingly pleasant environment without realizing that they need to improve.
- Neither caring nor challenging leads to manipulative insincerity, in which the individual is not challenged directly nor does their boss care personally about whether they perform well or progress.
- So, caring and challenging is the recommended combination.

EXERCISE: *Draw up a list of those that report to you and apply the process. Are there any problem areas? Draw up a list of bosses in the company and repeat the process. Are there any bosses whose approach falls into the three less desirable categories? If so, think about possible remedies.*

39

THE KNOWLEDGE
MASTERY GRID

- The Knowledge Mastery Grid maps self-awareness about personal knowledge levels with their reality.
- The vertical axis plots what an individual really knows about a subject – the degree to which they 'know what they're talking about,' or not, as the case may be.
- The horizontal axis plots the difference between people who think they know what they are talking about, and those who know that they don't know.
- This leads to very interesting typologies.
- Bottom left, the person does not know the subject matter, and knows that they don't know. As a result, they are humble and inquisitive, and keen to find out more. This person will not pretend that they do know.
- Top left, the individual actually knows a fair bit about the subject, but they don't really think that they do, which makes them underconfident, often leading to intense preparation for a meeting or conversation. This may stray into overpreparation.
- Bottom right, the person thinks they know what they are talking about, but they don't, so they tend to bullshit. They would be better off shutting up.
- Top right, the person does know a lot about the subject, and they know they do, which often leads to intellectual arrogance or just boring everyone else. Ideally, these people should calm down, say less and listen more.

REALLY KNOW
WHAT I AM TALKING ABOUT

(OVER) PREPARATION

UNDERCONFIDENCE

ARROGANCE

NEED TO CALM DOWN

DON'T THINK
I KNOW

THINK
I KNOW

FIND OUT

INQUISITIVE

BULLSHIT

NEED TO SHUT UP

DON'T REALLY KNOW

EXERCISE: *Choose a subject and analyse your own skills with the grid. Use the findings to work out whether you are under- or over-preparing for certain conversations or projects. If you fall on the right-hand side of the grid, consider toning it down a bit. Then use the technique to consider your colleagues and see what there is to learn about them.*

40

THE LEADERSHIP POTENTIAL GRID

	LAZY	HARD-WORKING
CLEVER	Make them a commander.	Make them a staff officer.
STUPID	You can always find something for them to do.	Fire them.

- The rather brilliantly named Kurt Von Hammerstein-Equord was the German Chief of the High Command. In 1934 he classified his officers into four classes based on whether they were clever, industrious (hard-working), lazy or stupid. He believed that each officer always possessed two of these qualities.

- If they were clever and hard-working, he appointed them to the General Staff.
- If they were stupid and lazy, you could always find something for them to do.
- If they were stupid and hard-working, he fired them because they were too dangerous.
- If they were clever and lazy, he put them into the highest posts because they had the mental clarity for difficult decisions and had the ability to make them by the easiest route.
- That's the moral of the story: the clever and lazy group are natural delegators and they always look for simpler, faster ways to get things done.

EXERCISE: *If you need to assess the leadership potential of people you are considering for promotion, try using the grid. It may seem a little fanciful, but it might throw up some interesting questions and offer an alternative, or complement, to other more modern methods of assessment.*

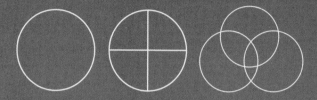

PART THREE

CIRCLES AND PIES

A WORD ON
CIRCLES
AND PIES

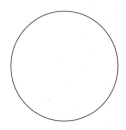

Stone circles. Crop circles. The circle of life. Hitting the bull's-eye.

Pies, fried eggs, onions, targets. Everyone loves a circle.

Circles offer the ability to handle huge amounts of data.

Quantities as a proportion of a greater whole are often easier to grasp as segments.

They are superb for highlighting subject matter and isolating elements.

Circles are complete in their own right, and so are ideal for concepts that need to be whole but do not need to specify direction.

Empty circles can be used to show overlap areas.

Circle size can represent volume or importance, and offer the chance to show satellite relationships.

It's an endless cycle of possibility.

41

THE TARGET, FRIED EGG OR ONION

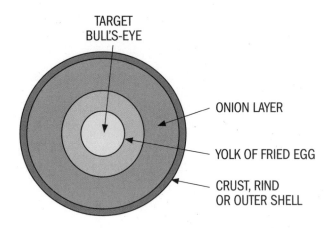

TARGET
BULL'S-EYE

ONION LAYER

YOLK OF FRIED EGG

CRUST, RIND
OR OUTER SHELL

- Simply drawing one circle inside another opens up a world of possibilities.
- The centre can be viewed as the yolk of an egg, the bull's-eye in a target, the core of an apple, or even the centre of the Earth.
- This can be taken to be the focal point of an issue, the essence, the inner workings, or the point of origin of something.

- In one version of the diagram, the outer area is seen as the circle of concern (all the stuff people are concerned about), whereas they should be concentrating on the circle of influence (the bit in the middle they can actually have a bearing on).
- The outer layer can also represent encasement, a broader world, or simply a larger pool of something – customers or the prospective size of an opportunity.
- Additional layers can then demonstrate gradation, as in the layers of an onion, or an outer shell such as the rind of a fruit.
- The width of each layer can be adjusted to represent the volume of the task, audience or issue in question.

EXERCISE: *Choose a subject where quantities need to be displayed. Draw a circle to represent the complete issue or number. Place a small circle at the core. Add layers as appropriate, taking time to consider their proportion in relation to each other. Try envisaging the diagram as a fruit, vegetable, target or other object that might inspire a useful title or analogy to articulate the issue.*

42

THE PIE CHART

- The Pie Chart is a classic way to represent data or segments of a larger whole.
- Usually each segment is proportional to its percentage – in this case 75%, 20% and 5%.
- If there are multiple segments, then the percentage quantity of each may need to be labelled numerically for clarity.
- Colouring each segment differently helps to give definition for a snapshot at a glance.
- If there are more than six segments the diagram will probably be too confusing and so another approach may be needed – probably a histogram.

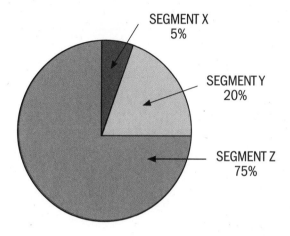

SEGMENT X
5%

SEGMENT Y
20%

SEGMENT Z
75%

EXERCISE: *Choose an issue where its quantity can be expressed in percentages. Try to have no more than six component parts. Convert the percentages into the correct volumes and show them as segments of the pie. Colour code and add descriptive numbers if helpful. Use the diagram to spark a new thought about how to view the issue.*

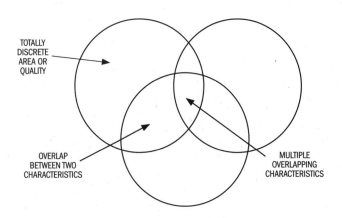

TOTALLY
DISCRETE
AREA OR
QUALITY

OVERLAP
BETWEEN TWO
CHARACTERISTICS

MULTIPLE
OVERLAPPING
CHARACTERISTICS

- Venn Diagrams were studied in detail by John Venn in 1880, although he called them Euler diagrams after Leonhard Euler who looked at them a century before.
- This is a highly flexible system of interlocking circles that are useful for identifying the contrast between overlapping qualities or areas of uniqueness.
- The minimum number of circles is two, and the maximum for most uses is three. (Highly advanced set theorists have gone as far as 16 intersections, but this is too complex for business purposes.)

- Once the circles are interlocked, totally discrete areas are revealed (in which there is no overlap). These can then be compared with the qualities of the overlap areas.
- Where three circles are used, the central area will show multiple overlapping characteristics.
- The volume of areas revealed should ideally be kept approximately proportional to their percentage of overlap so that the extent of the common ground is visually representative.

EXERCISE: *Choose two subjects with related but not identical properties. Arrange two circles to overlap in a proportion that accurately represents their degree of common ground. Also look at the discrete areas where there is no overlap. Make decisions based on the benefits of either common ground or uniqueness.*

SATELLITE SYSTEM

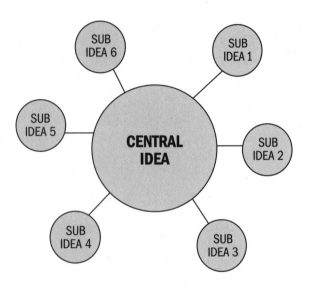

- The Central Idea Satellite System uses circles as representations of ideas or concepts, and links them together in a layout reminiscent of satellites orbiting around a central planet.
- The central idea or thought usually sits in the centre, and is represented by the largest circle on the diagram to denote its importance.

- Smaller satellites are then spun around it, normally a minimum of three and a suggested maximum of six.
- Thematically these satellite ideas should be related to the central thought.
- They could be variations on the theme, or different media through which it can be expressed, or different audiences receiving the message and so on, so long as all the orbiting thoughts are cousins in some way.
- This diagram looks simple enough, but it is not as easy as it looks to fill in. The satellites must be properly anchored themes that truly dramatize the fertility of the central idea. If they do not, then either choose ones that do or, in extreme cases, throw out the central idea in favour of a better one.

EXERCISE: *Identify a central thought and place it in the centre of the system. Draw up a list of related sub-themes. Arrange them in smaller bubbles around the central thought. If necessary, start a new diagram to display a different family of sub-thoughts. Use the diagram to demonstrate the breadth and application of the main theme.*

45

THE MOLECULAR STRUCTURE

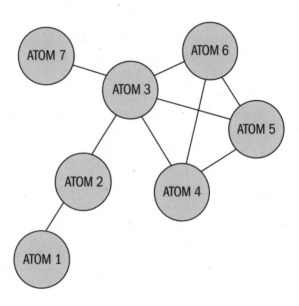

- The Molecular Structure takes its inspiration from the world of atoms and molecules.
- It is most useful for explaining the relationship between constituent parts of a more complex whole.

- It is particularly flexible inasmuch as it is not required to be uniform or symmetrical, and so can have an infinite number of constructions, with elements constantly being added or taken away.
- Each atom represents an element of the whole.
- As an example, imagine the diagram as a depiction of the components of a brand strategy, or perhaps an organization.
- The lines between each atom demonstrate some form of link. There may be only one link between one atom and another, as with atoms 1 and 2, or 3 and 7. Or there may be multiple links, as with the cluster of atoms 3, 4, 5 and 6.
- This enables the accurate depiction of individual or group links to reflect relationships or interrelationships.

EXERCISE: *Choose a subject, perhaps an organizational structure. Represent each component as a circle. Work out how they are related to each other by drawing a line connecting the parts that are linked. Re-draw the diagram if necessary to bring clarity to how it all works.*

46

THE WORK/LIFE BALANCE DIAGRAM

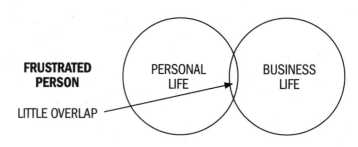

FRUSTRATED PERSON

LITTLE OVERLAP

PERSONAL LIFE

BUSINESS LIFE

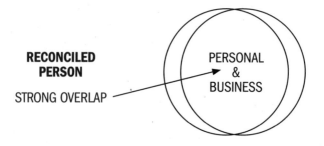

RECONCILED PERSON

STRONG OVERLAP

PERSONAL & BUSINESS

- This iteration of the Venn Diagram is helpful in determining whether you have a sensible work/life balance.
- The two circles represent your personal and business lives – that is to say the degree to which your character is broadly the same at work and in your spare time, and whether the nature of your work bears any relation to things that interest you in your spare time.
- Those with little overlap are leading two quite separate lives, and this often leads to frustration.
- Those with strong overlap tend to be better reconciled – not having to change their character at work, and generally working on things that interest them.

EXERCISE: *Use the two circles to depict your work and non-work character. Display the amount of overlap and try to make the degree of overlap proportional. Repeat if necessary for the nature of your work in relation to what interests you generally. If the overlap is small, work out your main frustration and see if you want to make some changes to your work or working hours.*

47

THE CHANGING ROLE OF THE TEAM LEADER CIRCLE

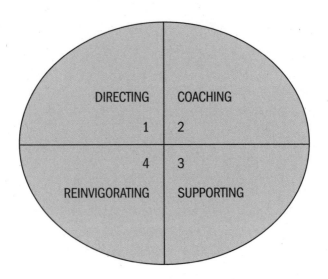

- The Changing Role of the Team Leader Circle is very helpful for working out how to deal with members of a team who may have different experience levels.
- In section one, the leader directs their subordinate, safe in the knowledge that they know what they are doing and can be left to it.

- In section two, the leader needs to coach the team member because they have not done the task before and need to be taught how to do it.
- In section three, the person knows pretty much what they are doing but may need some back-up, so the leader needs to perform a supporting role.
- In section four, the person has done the task so many times before that they need careful motivation, so the leader needs to reinvigorate their enthusiasm.
- It is important to note that the same individual might be in a different position for each of four different tasks, even on the same day, depending on their previous experience.

EXERCISE: *Choose a member of your team. Write down five or six tasks that you typically need them to carry out. Work out which state of affairs applies to your role as their team leader on each job. If you are unsure, ask them how comfortable they feel in carrying out the tasks. Repeat for each member of the team, and use it as a guide to your role when next delegating work.*

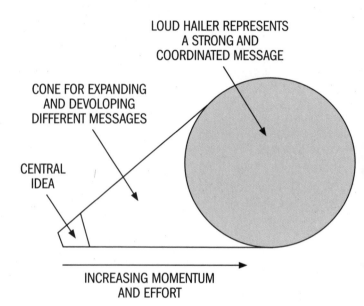

LOUD HAILER REPRESENTS
A STRONG AND
COORDINATED MESSAGE

CONE FOR EXPANDING
AND DEVOLOPING
DIFFERENT MESSAGES

CENTRAL
IDEA

INCREASING MOMENTUM
AND EFFORT

- The Cone or Loud Hailer is an interesting way to design a strategy for communication that involves multiple messages.
- The thin end or mouthpiece is a diagrammatic representation of the central idea.
- The body of the cone denotes the area in which the idea is expanded and developed into different versions of the message to suit different objectives and audiences.
- Momentum and effort should increase the more these messages are developed.
- The large circular opening on the right represents the full force of the coordinated campaign, in which all the individual messages combine to maximum effect.

EXERCISE: *Choose a communications campaign. Place the central idea to the left of the cone. Use the body of the cone to record all the different versions of the method required for different audiences or media. Have them come together as a coordinated whole on the far right.*

49 **THE SO WHAT?**
CYCLE OF QUESTIONS

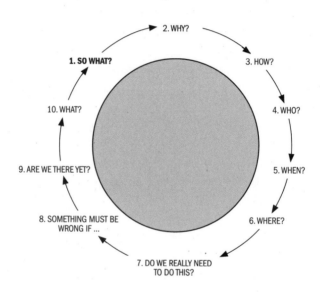

- The *So What?* Cycle of Questions is a useful ten-point process to make sure that ideas and projects actually get done.
- *So What?* is the initial screening question, effectively asking what the point of the project is. Assuming this is satisfactorily answered, then explaining why provides the rationale.

- The system then moves on to asking how, when and where the activity will get done, and who exactly will be doing it.
- Once all these elements have been thought through in a satisfactory way, there are a number of sense-check questions to make sure that nothing has been overlooked.
- These are *Do we really need to do this?*, *Something must be wrong if ...*(a sentence that requires completion), and *Are we there yet?*
- The *What?* question is left as a postscript at the end. If this hasn't been properly defined, then you may decide not to embark on the task at all.

EXERCISE: *Choose a project. Write down the ten questions. Answer each in sequence with a maximum of one sentence. If you cannot generate a satisfactory answer to a question, do not continue with the others. Instead consider whether to abandon or rethink the idea.*

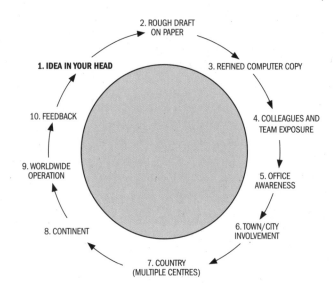

- The 'From Your Head to the World' circle is a system that helps you to work out how to get your thoughts across to others effectively.
- All ideas start in your head and the challenge is how to convey them as you intend.

- The first step is to commit a rough draft to paper, live with it for a while, and then produce a refined computer copy.
- The idea or thinking should then be test-driven on colleagues and team members before working out how to announce it in your office.
- The level of exposure thereafter depends on the scale of your operation, but could include town, city, country, continent or even worldwide communication.
- At each level there will be different considerations about how best to communicate, and the same method will not necessarily apply in every instance.

EXERCISE: *Select an idea that you need to reveal or share with others. Create a rough draft and then tidy it up. Test it out on some colleagues. Work out who else needs to understand, approve or enact it. Decide on a suitable method for best communicating at each level. Put the plan together and then enact it.*

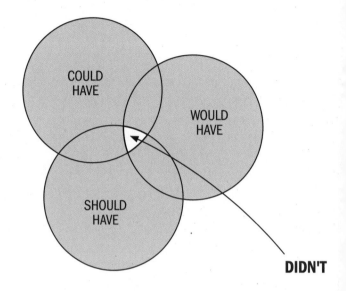

- Much has been written about how easy it is to have ideas. The world is full of them. It's getting them done that is far more of a challenge.
- Steve Jobs said, "*Real artists ship.*" In other words, they produce things, and then stand by for the reaction. Response is not always favourable, so shipping takes bravery.

- Not wishing to ship is effectively a fear of criticism, whether that's a musician still doing their 27th remix of a song, or a painter with a cellar full of work but no exhibition.
- Ideas have to be enacted, otherwise technically they have no tangible existence.
- Overcoming the resistance, as Seth Godin calls it, takes bravery and energy.
- "*Could have*," "*would have*," and "*should have*" don't cut it. They just mean that you didn't.

EXERCISE: *Take some time to review all the things that you would ideally like to do, whether work or personal. Include all your dreams and half-baked ideas. Now consider how much you really want to do them. If there is something that you really want to do, work out what your resistance to doing it is. Now consider how to remove the blockage. There's probably nothing stopping you.*

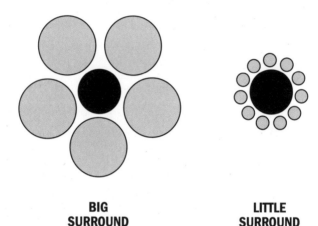

**BIG
SURROUND**

**LITTLE
SURROUND**

- This diagram is an optical illusion. The dark circles in the centre of each are the same size, but the surrounding lighter circles confuse us into thinking that the one on the right is larger.
- The name of this illusion comes from the 19th-century German psychologist Hermann Ebbinghaus, who pioneered studies of cognition and memory.
- Dr Jessica Witt of Purdue University had these images projected onto golf holes, and then watched the results unfold. Those golfers who faced the "little surround" on the right sank twice as many putts as the others.

- This effectively shows that performance can be affected by perception. So, next time you are faced with a tricky task, you can use this visualization technique to perceive it as large and inviting rather than small and forbidding.
- Life isn't a game of golf, but perception of a challenge can certainly affect performance.

EXERCISE: *Choose a difficult task, project or challenge. Imagine a visual image that sums up what is at stake or what needs to be achieved. Either use your imagination or a sketchpad to envisage how it can be viewed in a less scary way, or in a more attainable form.*

THE GOLDEN CIRCLE

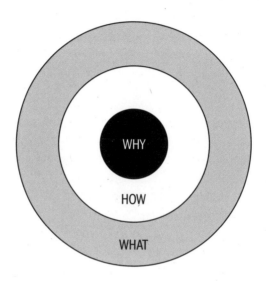

- In his book *Start With Why*, Simon Sinek introduces the Golden Circle, with *why* in the middle, then *how*, then *what* on the outside.
- The sequence is important because it's the reverse of what happens in most companies, who can easily say what they do, and sometimes how, but rarely why they do it.
- In fact, it doesn't so much matter *what* you do in business – it matters *why* you do it.

- The sequence mirrors how the brain works – with the limbic brain in the centre responsible for our feelings (why), and the neocortex performing rational functions (what).
- Business leaders can inspire everyone to take action when they start with *why*.
- Companies need clarity, discipline and consistency to stick to their *why*, and this becomes their true authenticity, unlike other companies who hilariously ask their customers how they can 'be more authentic.'

EXERCISE: *Choose a suitable subject, such as your company, department or a major project. Write down 'what' it does (this should be fairly straightforward). Now explain 'how' it does it (possibly harder). Now articulate 'why' it does it. This last one could be difficult. If there is no answer forthcoming, examine your purpose in detail. Without a clear one, people could be working in the absence of a decent reason, leading to poor motivation.*

THE IDEAL TEAM PLAYER
VENN DIAGRAM

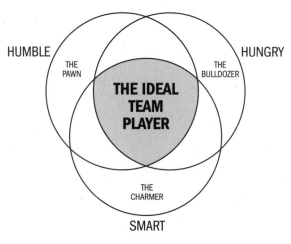

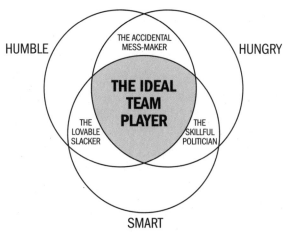

- Again according to Patrick Lencioni, there are three essential virtues that make someone the ideal team player:
- *Humble*: humility is the single greatest and most indispensable attribute.
- *Hungry*: these people are self-motivated and diligent.
- *Smart*: these people demonstrate common sense when dealing with others (it's not the same as intellectual smartness).
- Those with just one are fairly easy to spot:
- *Humble only* = the pawn, who often gets left out.
- *Hungry only* = the bulldozer, who often annoys everyone else.
- *Smart only* = the charmer, with great social skills but low contribution.
- Those with 2 out of 3 are much harder to identify:
- *Humble and hungry* = the accidental mess-maker, unaware of their effect on people.
- *Humble and smart* = the lovable slacker, who only does as much as asked.
- *Hungry and smart* = the skillful politician, out for their own benefit.

EXERCISE: *Apply the technique to analyse hiring new staff, assessing current employees, developing those who are lacking in one or more of the virtues, or looking at your organization's culture. Choose a team, examine their qualities, and plot them on the diagram. Use the analysis to promote understanding of who is performing what role.*

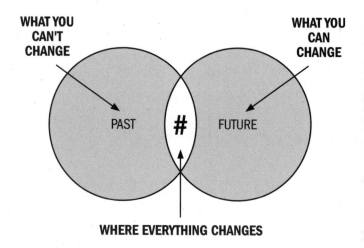

WHAT YOU CAN'T CHANGE

WHAT YOU CAN CHANGE

PAST # FUTURE

WHERE EVERYTHING CHANGES

- According to Max McKeown in his book *#Now*, you can't change the past, but you can change the future, and now is where everything can be changed.
- *Nowists* love moving and seek joy in doing things; they don't waste their lives seeking happiness, so they seek it now; they make rapid, effortless decisions; they see sequences, and have a sense of where they are going; they are hard to stop and a force of nature; they are self-trusting, confident in their abilities and have do-it energy.

- If you learn to embrace your haste, and love your *Nowist* nature, you can discover effortless action and decisions, embrace opportunities, obstacles and crises, and keep moving forward in a thoroughly positive way.
- Those living in the past are called *Thenist* – they suffer from loss, regret and worry. *Nowists* are more likely to achieve growth, joy and reward.

EXERCISE: *We live in the present but carry the anxieties of the past and concerns about the future with us at all times. Envisage a task or situation. Remove all baggage by breaking with the past. Forget the future too – it will come soon enough. Then work out precisely what your approach to this issue is right now. Now do that.*

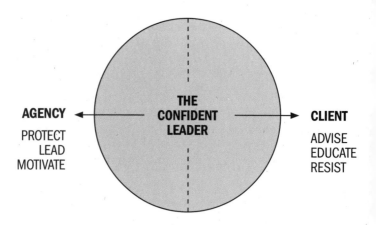

- Anyone working in a service industry (over 80% of the Gross Domestic Product of both the UK and the USA) will often be strung between the customer and what their company can realistically do.
- In this respect, anyone in sales, account management, customer service, and scores of other roles are effectively the gatekeeper of the relationship between the customer and the company.

- It's a tricky place to be, and can leave the individual torn between the two sides, somewhat like the Roman god Janus, who is usually depicted with two faces, one facing the past and the other the future (hence January).
- Confident leaders need to become comfortable with this apparent contradiction.
- Looking outwards, they should advise and educate customers, while resisting unreasonable demands.
- Looking inwards, they should protect, lead and motivate their staff so that they can provide an excellent service, without fear.

EXERCISE: *Consider the nature of your, or your company's, relationship with the customer. Imagine your role as double-sided. Separate the apparent contradiction between the two perspectives. Then draw up an approach for each view. Now understand the dual nature of the job for yourself, or explain it to colleagues.*

THE DISMAYED DESIGNER'S
VENN DIAGRAM

HOW WOULD YOU LIKE YOUR GRAPHIC DESIGN?

(YOU MAY PICK TWO)

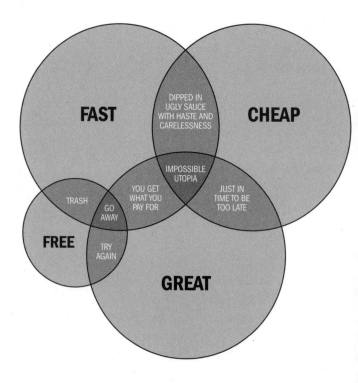

- This is a relatively unusual 4-way Venn Diagram (most have two or three circles). It deals with the time-honoured problem of customers or clients making demands on their suppliers or agencies. Ignoring for a moment the small free one, the elements are always the same in these conversations, just as they are in The IF Triangle: quality, price and timing.
- As ever, you can only have two out of the three variables. Good and cheap won't be fast. Fast and good won't be cheap. Cheap and fast won't be good. So what do you want? It is one of the most powerful lines of argument in any negotiation.
- Enjoy the humour of this one.

EXERCISE: Although humorous, it is possible to derive serious benefit from this diagram. Consider any unreasonable request from a customer or client. Work through the quality, price and timing variables carefully. Either ask them which two elements they want or decide yourself which two they need. State your timing requirements and price accordingly.

GREY AREA

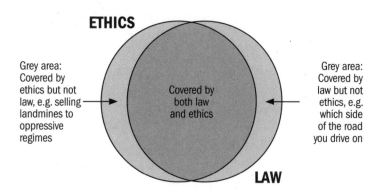

ETHICS

Grey area: Covered by ethics but not law, e.g. selling landmines to oppressive regimes

Covered by both law and ethics

Grey area: Covered by law but not ethics, e.g. which side of the road you drive on

LAW

- This Venn Diagram looks simple enough, but the subject matter it contains is anything but. It features in a weighty textbook called *Business Ethics*.
- Having described how business ethics deals with right and wrong, it poses the question: surely the law is also about issues of right and wrong? As you can see, the answer is: not always.

- The law is a codification of ethics institutionalized into specific social rules, regulations and proscriptions, but the two are not equivalent. The best way to think about this is to use the diagram. For example, selling landmines to oppressive regimes is covered by ethics but not law. Which side of the road you drive on is covered by law but not ethics. The rest is up for discussion.
- Interestingly by the fifth edition of the book, the diagram had been updated to the one here, which suggests that ethics and the law had considerably extended its reach in the intervening decade.

EXERCISE: Consider an ethical dilemma that you or your business faces. Work out whether you are dealing with ethics, the law or both. Then make a decision or take legal advice.

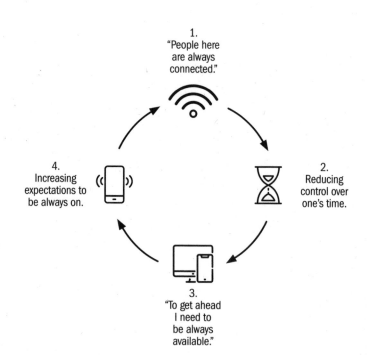

1.
"People here
are always
connected."

2.
Reducing
control over
one's time.

3.
"To get ahead
I need to
be always
available."

4.
Increasing
expectations to
be always on.

- This is taken from a book called *Indistractable*, by Nir Eyal, and attempts to encapsulate how workplace technology 'drives us crazy.' The author claims it was inspired by a book by Leslie Perlow, a Professor of Leadership at Harvard Business School. There were different versions of her book, variously titled *Sleeping With Your Smart Phone/Cell Phone/Blackberry*.
- The death spiral starts when a company claims something like "People here are always connected." This reduces individual control over their time. Meanwhile people have a nagging suspicion that if they want to get ahead then they need to be always available, which in turn increases expectations that they will be 'always on.'
- The best one can say about this is that the loop has to be broken.

EXERCISE: *Look at the loop. Does it resonate with how you work and your relationship with technology? If so, choose an access point and break the loop.*

NAMES PIE CHART

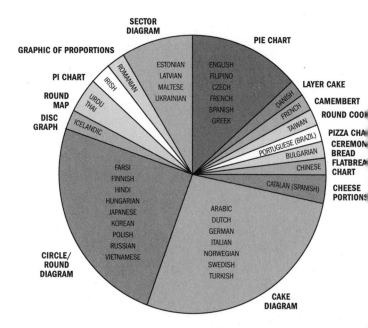

SECTOR DIAGRAM
GRAPHIC OF PROPORTIONS
PI CHART
ROUND MAP
DISC GRAPH
ROMANIAN
IRISH
URDU
THAI
ICELANDIC
ESTONIAN
LATVIAN
MALTESE
UKRAINIAN
ENGLISH
FILIPINO
CZECH
FRENCH
SPANISH
GREEK
PIE CHART
LAYER CAKE
CAMEMBERT
ROUND COOK
DANISH
FRENCH
TAIWAN
PORTUGUESE (BRAZIL)
BULGARIAN
CHINESE
CATALAN (SPANISH)
PIZZA CHA
CEREMON
BREAD
FLATBREA
CHART
CHEESE
PORTIONS
FARSI
FINNISH
HINDI
HUNGARIAN
JAPANESE
KOREAN
POLISH
RUSSIAN
VIETNAMESE
ARABIC
DUTCH
GERMAN
ITALIAN
NORWEGIAN
SWEDISH
TURKISH
CIRCLE/ROUND DIAGRAM
CAKE DIAGRAM

- To end this part on Circles and Pies, here is a monster pie chart that attempts to categorize what different languages call... a pie chart. There are quite a few of these in existence, but this version is based on one created by Eric Hittinger, Public Policy Professor at Rochester Institute of Technology.

- This author was first alerted to this phenomenon when the French translation of *The Diagrams Book* returned containing this:

LE CAMEMBERT

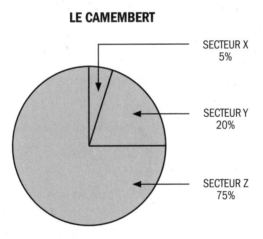

SECTEUR X
5%

SECTEUR Y
20%

SECTEUR Z
75%

EXERCISE: *Think carefully about the cultural backgrounds of the people with whom you work.*

PART FOUR

TIMELINES AND YEAR VIEWS

A WORD ON
TIMELINES
AND YEAR VIEWS

Time – a concept invented by man to stop everything happening at once.

Lines of time can be divided in scores of different ways.

Breaking the year into different sizes of time can be revealing.

Strategy, energy and motivation can all be seen in a new way.

And individuals and companies might even find it easier to hit their deadlines.

THE LIVELINE

INITIATE   COMPLETE

                                            DEADLINE

                    LIVELINE

←——————————————————————→

        CONCENTRATE   IGNORE

- A deadline is a time limit for any activity.
- The biggest mistake that everybody makes when dealing with deadlines is to concentrate on the deadline rather than the bit that comes before.
- The liveline should be 99% longer than the deadline.
- The length of a deadline, or moment of launch, will depend on the length of the liveline. For example, a one-hour liveline might have a one-minute deadline, whereas a five year project might take one day to reveal.

- So once you have allocated the deadline, don't spend any more time concentrating on it.
- Decide the deadline, initiate the project, and then spend all your time concentrating on the liveline that constitutes 99% of the work required.

EXERCISE: Choose a project. Work out the amount of time it will take. Define the duration and nature of the deadline. Now work backwards, concentrating on the liveline. Concentrate on the length of it, and plan what needs to be done at sensible intervals long before the deadline.

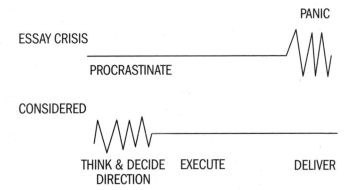

- The Personal Deadline examines the problem that most people leave things too late before they start a task.
- For most people this was a habit they acquired at college when faced with a deadline for handing in an essay or dissertation.
- Common sense suggests that a measured approach over the time available would yield a less stressed run-up and a higher quality result, but human nature dictates otherwise and many leave everything to the last minute.
- This timeline helps to focus the mind on the task ahead while there is still plenty of time.

- The considered line shows that it pays to examine as much of the material and as many of the important issues as early as possible.
- In this approach, all the important decision makers gather as fast as possible to judge the most suitable direction. At this stage, this is probably a guesstimate that is 80% right.
- Once direction is decided, then orderly execution of the work can be embarked on, with completion being achieved smoothly. If by any chance information then comes in that contradicts the original direction, there is still time to course correct.
- The idea is to avoid an Essay Crisis in which the thinking phase is left too late and hasty work is crammed in at the very end under unnecessary time pressure. The old cliché "I work better under pressure" is false and misleading.

EXERCISE: Choose a project with a known deadline, preferably no less than one week away. Work backwards from the due date to work out how much effort will be needed to complete it. Decide direction immediately, or no later than tomorrow. Initiate the execution in an orderly fashion over the remaining time.

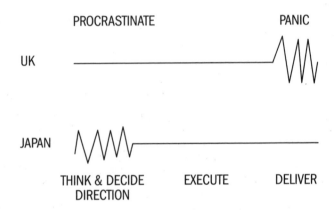

- This Cultural Deadline demonstrates that different cultures approach deadlines in different ways.
- Consider this diagram as a hypothetical timeline for the launch of a product being manufactured and marketed by the Japanese and the British. The two countries are just examples.
- The Japanese line shows them grappling with their problems early, deciding direction and moving out of the thinking phase as quickly as possible, and in plenty of time to deliver.
- The UK line shows them panicking at the last moment having failed to tackle the hard stuff early.

- The second approach is more likely to produce an excellent product on time because it adheres to the philosophy of *"Do the worst first."*
- This is because if something unexpected crops up, there is still time to deal with it without affecting the deadline.
- It also allows slippage time in which to make mistakes, pursue lines of inquiry that do not ultimately prove fruitful, change your mind, or simply have a better idea.

EXERCISE: *Choose a significant project. Examine the cultural tendencies in your company. Consider the approaches of all the parties involved. Anticipate those who are likely to be inclined to procrastinate. Devise a plan that deals with the difficult decisions as early in the timeline as possible.*

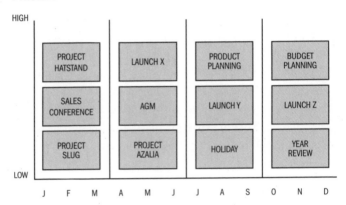

ACTIVITY
PRIORITY

HIGH

PROJECT HATSTAND	LAUNCH X	PRODUCT PLANNING	BUDGET PLANNING
SALES CONFERENCE	AGM	LAUNCH Y	LAUNCH Z
PROJECT SLUG	PROJECT AZALIA	HOLIDAY	YEAR REVIEW

LOW

J F M A M J J A S O N D

- The Year to a View is a classic calendar diagram.
- It represents the Gregorian calendar that was officially introduced by Pope Gregory XIII in 1582.
- As such, it is divided into twelve months in an attempt to reflect the equinoxes, which is perfectly fine but doesn't necessarily mean it is a helpful timeline for businesses.

- For better or worse, all the businesses in the world use a Year to a View to represent their financial performance (the financial year), and most divide the year into four quarters, or periods of three months.
- While these dictate the content of the horizontal axis, all sorts of different variables can be used on the vertical.
- In this instance, the vertical criterion is priority of project importance, and they have been spread over the four quarters in sequence.
- The diagram is probably the universally recognized way of seeing a year's activity at a glance.

EXERCISE: *Choose a year-long time period. Choose a subject for the vertical axis. Place the subject matter in sequence throughout the year. Use the result as a planning tool to anticipate timings and resource needs.*

YEAR VIEW

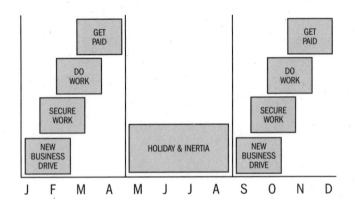

- The Tertials v. Quarters Year View provides an alternative way of carving up the year.
- In many businesses, quarters are unsatisfactory units of time because they are slightly too short to provide a helpful view of what is happening.

- A tertial is a four-month view designed to allow a business to initiate a new business drive in the first month, secure some work in the second, do the work in the third, and get paid in the fourth, thereby concluding a proper cycle of work that can be planned effectively or analysed afterwards.
- Mapping the year in this way often reveals different findings than when using conventional quarters.
- For example, the summer tertial from May to August will almost certainly be less productive than the other two. This phasing may be different in particularly seasonal businesses.

EXERCISE: *Take your current year view, which is almost certainly divided into quarters. Recast the shape using tertials instead. If your business has a particular seasonal pattern move the start dates of the tertials to the months that make the most sense. Consider whether it might be more helpful to plan the year like this in future.*

PRODUCTIVE:	6 MONTHS (ABOVE AVERAGE)
UNDERPRODUCTIVE:	6 MONTHS (BELOW AVERAGE)
DECISION WINDOWS (D):	M/M/S
CRISIS BOMBS (*):	J/A/A

- The Less-Than-Twelve-Month Year is a diagram that makes a philosophical point about activity, or the lack of it at certain times, in companies.
- On the surface, businesses are active for twelve months a year, but in truth there are plenty of periods when they are not very productive, and this diagram helps to work out when those times are likely to be.
- All businesses have different rhythms, but in this example the most productive (above average periods) are in March, May and September.

- In these 'decision windows,' every important decision maker is present, things get decided, and they get done.
- From time to time, 'crisis bombs' go off – unexpected developments that are unhelpful (in this example, this happens in January, April and August). They take up a lot of time and energy and deflect the company from its normal work, making its performance below average.
- By looking at the pattern of previous years, most of these events can be predicted and allowed for. Often this tallies with simple holiday patterns, but not always.
- Viewing the year in this way usually shows that the 'twelve month year' is almost always 'shorter' than you think.

EXERCISE: *Look at the year ahead. Predict the likely highly productive periods, and the unproductive ones. If necessary, predict when the decision windows and crisis bombs will occur. Now add up the truly productive months and consider reviewing any forecasts and resource planning you have undertaken.*

67 THE STRATEGY V. TACTICS YEAR VIEW

OVERARCHING THOUGHT (THE STRATEGY)

EXAMPLES AND PROOF (TACTICS)

TACTIC 1	TACTIC 2	TACTIC 3	TACTIC 4

J F M A M J J A S O N D

- One of the trickiest things businesses struggle with is the difference between strategy and tactics, and how to plan their shape.
- The Strategy v. Tactics Year View helps to clarify matters.
- The strategy is the overarching thought, here shown as a top block or lintel. This is the consistent theme and direction that never varies, and against which all other activities can be judged and measured.

- In some models, this is shown as a foundation. Both are acceptable, so long as their components remain constant.
- With strategy, it's not what changes that matters – it's what stays the same. Because people like novelty, the temptation is to fiddle with everything, but it takes courage *not* to change something.
- The tactics are specific examples or proof of the strategy, and their deployment must have a clear beginning and end.
- The year view helps clearly distinguish the two elements, and enables you to map out precisely when the tactical initiatives should occur.

EXERCISE: *Look at the year ahead. Decide on the overall strategy and place it as a constant overarching theme. Choose an appropriate number of tactics and place them in the right time segment. Look at the total picture and decide if it is suitably balanced. Use the year view to explain the plan to colleagues.*

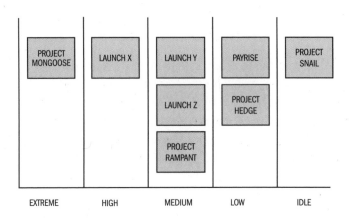

ENERGY LEVEL

- The Energy Line was suggested in 2010 by Scott Belsky in his book *Making Ideas Happen*.
- Most companies and their staff have far too many projects on the go at once, and as such their most precious commodity is energy because they only have a finite amount of it and can't do everything at the same time.

- The idea is to place your projects along an Energy Line according to how much energy they should receive, as in the diagram.
- It is important to note that this categorization is not based on how much time you are spending on a project – energy now is not the same as time in total over a project lifespan.
- Classifying your work this way prompts questions about the degree to which you are focusing on the right things.

EXERCISE: *Draw up a list of all your projects. Place each one in one of the categories, from extreme to idle. Remember to concentrate on energy level, not time spent. Move them around until the priority is right. Repeat the process as often as is necessary depending on the number and average duration of your projects.*

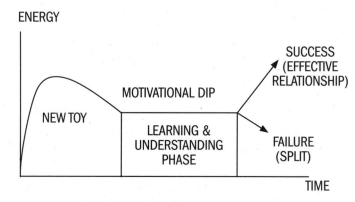

- The Motivational Dip is another way of looking at energy and application of resources. It can be used to analyse just one project or an entire relationship.
- It looks at enthusiasm over time, and can be used to predict the moments when things are likely to lose momentum and slip.
- The vertical axis represents amount of energy devoted to a task or relationship.
- The horizontal time axis maps the stages that motivation levels will probably go through.

- Things typically start well with a 'new toy' mentality – the honeymoon phase.
- A Motivational Dip is usually experienced before a more settled learning and understanding phase kicks in.
- After this, the project either moves on to success and completion, or fizzles out in failure.
- The relationship version of this final phase will determine whether two parties working together, such as a client and their agency, will establish an effective relationship or split up.

EXERCISE: *Choose a project or relationship that is just about to start. Plot the likely phases and work out when the Motivational Dip is likely to occur. Put measures in place to counteract it. You can also apply the method retrospectively to see when things went wrong and learn how to improve matters in the future.*

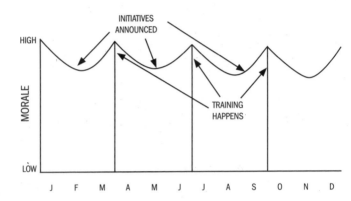

- The Motivational Clothes Line enables managers and especially Human Resources managers to plan and pace initiatives to optimum effect throughout the year.
- The vertical axis represents staff morale, and naturally we want this to be as high as possible as often as possible.
- The peaks, or tops of the clothes line poles, represent the moments of highest morale, and these coincide with training initiatives or other efforts that the company makes to help staff.
- Not surprisingly, this declines over time after the event.

- The knack for managers is to predict the point at which this should fall no lower lest it become detrimental. This is precisely when the next initiative should be announced, thus sending morale upward again in anticipation of the event.
- By planning the year in this way, managers can ensure that morale never falls below a certain level, and can avoid criticism that the company is doing nothing for their staff, since at any given moment something has just happened, or is going to soon.

EXERCISE: *Plot the minimum and maximum realistic morale levels for the year. Choose a suitable number of initiatives that will improve matters. Space them appropriately throughout the year. Use the Motivational Clothes Line to strike the right balance between the number of events and their effect on morale levels.*

9.00 ------- 1.00 ------- 6.00

- The bar code provides a visual depiction of a day filled with hundreds of short, bitty tasks. This is not usually through the choice of the person doing the work. It's because they keep being interrupted.
- When that happens, it takes the average person 12 to 15 minutes to get back to doing what they were doing. So if they are disturbed more than four times an hour, they have lost their whole career.
- Studies now show that multitasking doesn't work. If you want to produce proper high quality work, you need to allocate a decent run of time for each task, without interruption.
- Planning your day more like the version on the right means you can complete fulfilling tasks on your own terms.
- This includes suitable breaks, and controlled use of email and other technology so that you can really concentrate on what truly matters.

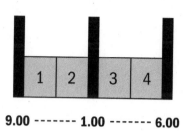

9.00 ------- **1.00** ------- **6.00**

EXERCISE: Look at your diary planner for the day, or week. Correlate the time available with the nature of the tasks you want to do. Earmark important jobs that require high quality thinking, estimate the time needed, and block out the necessary run of time. When enacting these, go somewhere where no one can find you, and do not take any technology with you. If needed, allocate shorter chunks of time for rapid administrivia or email.

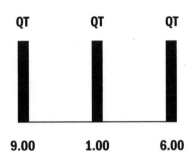

- There's no time like today, so it pays to work out how you are going to use it. The Day Shape Organizer helps you do that.
- First, we need to distinguish between two types of work: quantitative and qualitative. Quantitative work can neither be done well nor badly – it's just stuff that needs to be churned through. Qualitative work requires more time and absolutely needs to be of high quality.
- So now you can plan your day in a new way based on the quantitative (QT) versus qualitative (QL) distinction. Start by allocating short bursts of quantitative time, in which you will knock over a lot of small tasks in one burst. Try not to do this more than three times a day, and never for longer than 30 minutes per session.

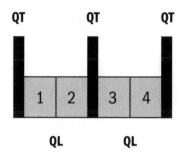

- Then map out decent runs of time, usually a minimum of an hour, to do some proper thinking or creating. Interlock them with the quantitative bursts, and don't mix up the two types of work.

EXERCISE: *Plan your day in a new way based on the quantitative (QT) versus qualitative (QL) distinction. Review this blend based on your personal style, depending on whether you are a morning or evening person.*

THE BALANCED WEEK ORGANIZER

8 HOURS

M   T   W   T   F

- If your weeks usually look like this, then you are in trouble. You'll never keep it up, and we know that many people exceed eight hours a day. You need The Balanced Week Organizer.
- You need to plan thinking and planning times into your week to pause, reflect and plan again.
- Even the week on the right looks pretty packed, but at least there is some breathing space to catch up and recover.

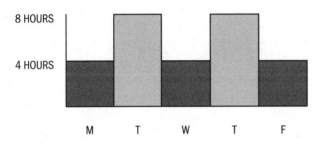

8 HOURS

4 HOURS

M   T   W   T   F

EXERCISE: *Review the last few weeks and map out what your workload was like. If it was packed, design a week that includes thinking time as well as just action. Remove as many meetings as possible and block out planning and thinking time. Protect it ferociously in your diary.*

74 THE GARTNER HYPE CYCLE

- The Gartner Hype Cycle was invented by the information technology company Gartner to represent how technology products usually move through a series of phases. They admit that it's not perfect but the shape is often right.
- A potential technology breakthrough starts it off, even if an actual product doesn't exist yet. There is a peak of inflated expectations, usually involving a mixture of success and failure stories.
- Interest then wanes and products often fail to deliver. Some entrants even leave the market - that's the trough – until second- and third-generation products make improvements and the benefits are more widely understood.
- In the plateau of productivity, mainstream adoption takes place.

EXERCISE: Look at a market and plot the introduction of a new technology or product. What shape and duration did it follow? Consider a new product you are considering launching into a market. What pattern is it likely to follow? What timespan? Will it be viable? Repeat multiple times to envisage a range of scenarios.

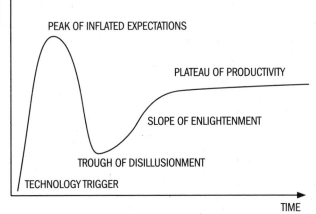

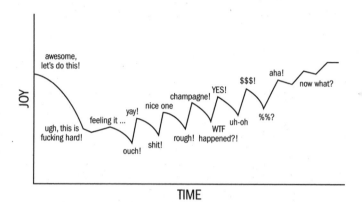

- The Messy Middle was described by Scott Belsky in his book of the same name. He pointed out that we celebrate starts and finishes, but rarely discuss the messy journey in between, where odds are defied and great teams and products are ultimately made. The middle may not be pretty, but it is illuminating. It's where you realize what you are capable of, and how resilient people can be.

- The map, not surprisingly, shows the initial dip as the complexity of the task becomes apparent. What then happens is a series of small victories over difficulty that eventually rises to a successful conclusion. The author describes this as a cycle of: start, endure, optimize, finish, then repeat.
- This model could help teams and businesses to take a more realistic view of how a project is likely to unfold.

EXERCISE: Choose a project that is soon to begin. Instead of writing a conventional block plan that itemizes tasks in a sequence, try anticipating all the dips and problems that may well happen. Plot that as a series of troughs and peaks, and see if that informs a different approach to the project, workflow, motivation, timing or resource allocation.

THE RATIONAL DROWNING SELLING TECHNIQUE

- This is a selling technique reinterpreted as a timeline graphic. The original concept comes from a book called *The Challenger Sale* by Dixon and Adamson which summarized a study of 6,000 salespeople and their approaches. Rational drowning refers to the moment when a rational approach (data, evidence, etc.) is used to reframe the argument or customer request from what they thought was the issue to something else.
- This usually quantifies the true, often hidden cost of the problem or the size of the opportunity they had completely overlooked. The drowning element refers to the moment when the customer suddenly worries about the size of the task or their lack of understanding of the issue.

- This graphic merely expresses that moment as part of a sales process. The time scale could be as short as a revelatory moment in a presentation, or as long as months before the customer or prospect emerges on the right side to a successful conclusion.
- In plain English, this might be phrased along the lines of: *"You certainly have an issue/opportunity with X, but did you know you also have an issue/opportunity with Y and Z? Here's the evidence."*
- Then at the appropriate moment, help them out of the drowning phase to a better place.

EXERCISE: *Look at a sales presentation or process that is coming up. Instead of just diving in and selling what you have to offer, or using the same old presentation, consider the pacing of this technique. Is the task as currently seen really all that's involved? What information might make the issue or opportunity much bigger or multi-faceted? Use that to build a better-informed case.*

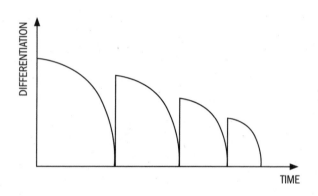

- Another contribution from Peterson & Riesterer in *Conversations That Win the Complex Sale* is this recurring shark's fin, and here's the story behind it. If you study differentiation over time, you can see that when an innovation comes out, the company behind it can benefit for a while, but it doesn't last forever. There's a finite window in which to reap the rewards, but when competitors catch up, that advantage disappears.

- So the idea is to look at the next innovation and the one after that, to keep this sequence of advantage going. You'll notice though that the fins get smaller as time passes, with the authors challenging you to 'stay ahead of the shark'.

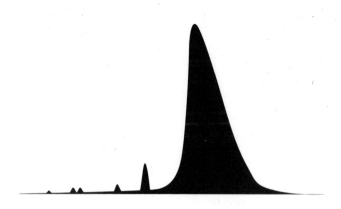

- Of course, you could argue that any company is lucky to have one shark's fin, let alone several. More common is a relatively flat market status quo, followed by a sudden burst of popularity, and then a return to entropy.

EXERCISE: Look at your category, sector, market or product range. What is the typical shape of growth and decline? Map out the sequence of shark fins, or just one, and try to make the shape as accurate as possible to reality, with a timeline along the bottom. Use the modelling to predict outcomes in your field and plan accordingly.

1% worse every day for one year. $0.99^{365} = 00.03$
1% better every day for one year. $1.01^{365} = 37.78$

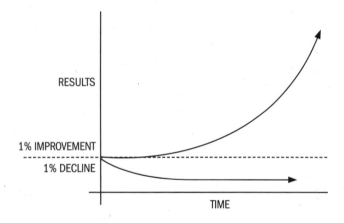

RESULTS

1% IMPROVEMENT

1% DECLINE

TIME

- We finish this chapter with a rapid-fire trio of time-based concepts from *Atomic Habits*, by the aptly named James Clear. His overall point is that tiny changes can lead to remarkable results.
- This curve shows that the effects of small habits compound over time. If you get 1% better at something each day, you'll end up with results that are nearly 37 times better after one year. It's a serious piece of maths.

EXERCISE: *No action required, other than to absorb the point about compound improvement and consider developing a new habit that would be more beneficial for you.*

79 THE PLATEAU OF LATENT POTENTIAL

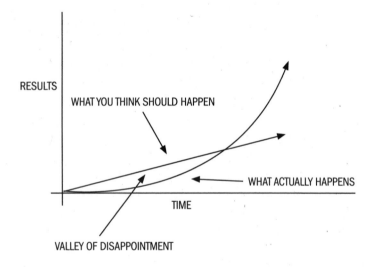

RESULTS

WHAT YOU THINK SHOULD HAPPEN

WHAT ACTUALLY HAPPENS

TIME

VALLEY OF DISAPPOINTMENT

- The second timeline from James Clear. This is all about expectation versus reality. We often expect progress to be linear, but it isn't. The results of your efforts are often delayed.
- This tends to lead to a valley of disappointment where people feel discouraged after putting in a lot of hard work without experiencing any results. However, this work is rarely wasted – merely being stored to show its benefit at some later point. This is similar to the Motivational Dip.

EXERCISE: Consider an effort you are making to reduce a bad habit or increase a good one. Plot the likely timeline to represent when you believe you will start to see a difference. Now build in a suitable delay, plus the valley of disappointment, and regard the time in between as your plateau of latent potential.

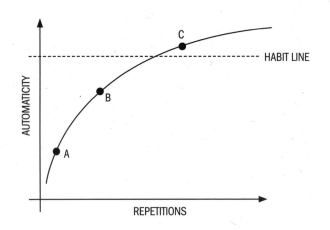

- And finally, a third piece of wisdom from James Clear, a schematic which explains how habits are formed.
- In the beginning (A) a habit requires a lot of effort and concentration to perform. After some repetitions (B) it becomes easier but still needs some conscious attention. By the time you have done it many times (C) it becomes more automatic than conscious. Beyond this stage (the habit line) it can be done more or less without thinking and a new habit has been formed.

EXERCISE: *More of an attitude than an exercise. Try to apply the discipline that sticks with a new (good) habit until it becomes automatic – push through to the habit line.*

PART FIVE

FLOWS AND CONCEPTS

A WORD ON
FLOWS
AND CONCEPTS

Some ideas need flow. They may need to meander.

Work needs to flow in organizations, and people need to know how it's going to work.

Flows certainly need to demonstrate movement.

They can be temporal. Or directional. Or suggestive of a process of some kind.

They can also represent processes of the mind – concepts.

Rivers, dams, funnels, hoppers and buckets. If it's to do with water it might help an idea along.

HOW TO DO IT

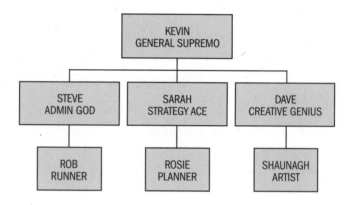

- An organization chart needs to be crystal clear.
- Its purpose is to explain to the people represented in it how they are supposed to interact with their colleagues. It should also be capable of explaining to a potential client how a company is organized.
- A clear chart should allow anyone looking at it to work out the basic hierarchy based on who is the boss, who is the next subordinate down and so on. These boxes should be linked with clear vertical lines.

- Descriptions of what role the individuals perform can be added if it helps, or the entire process can be carried out just for department functions rather than people and roles.
- Dotted lines do not work because they cause confusion about who reports to whom.
- Cross-reports and multiple bosses should also be avoided.

EXERCISE: *Either choose an existing organization chart or start from scratch. Work out who reports to whom in a simple hierarchy. Map it out with vertical lines. Add job descriptions if necessary. Avoid cross-reports, dotted lines and multiple bosses. Use the chart to clarify roles, or to identify relationships that are simply too complex.*

HOW NOT TO DO IT

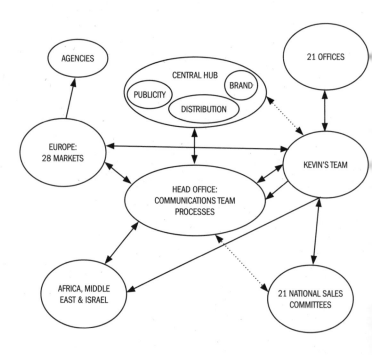

- This is a chart I was once given to 'explain' how an advertising agency worked with an international client. If anybody can understand how it works, do please get in touch.
- Organization charts are a major culprit when it comes to the golden rule of diagrams – that their primary purpose is to clarify and inform.
- This diagram has a number of faults.
- First, it contains 11 circles, which is too much.
- Second, it contains 12 arrows, which is also too much.
- Third, it contains circles within a circle, for no apparent reason.
- Fourth, it contains dotted lines, which always cause confusion.
- Fifth, there has been no attempt to relate the scale of the circles to the size of the individual or division.

EXERCISE: Select a complex set of interrelationships, or find a confusing organization chart. Strip out as many components as possible. Analyse every arrow to work out what it is trying to communicate. If there is simply too much information on the chart, break it down into two or three clearer ones.

THE THREE BUCKETS

**BRILLIANT
BASICS**

**COMPELLING
DIFFERENCE**

**CHANGING
THE GAME**

- The Three Buckets exercise was introduced by Adam Morgan in his book *The Pirate Inside* in 2004.
- It is an extremely helpful way to categorize projects and work out how effective they are likely to be.
- Each project must be placed in one of the three buckets.
- On the left is Brilliant Basics. These represent "excellence as standard." You or your company should be doing these well as a matter of course, just like your competitors.

- In the middle is "Compelling Difference." These should be "significantly better than normal." These are demonstrably better than your competitors, but not genuinely remarkable.
- On the right is Changing the Game. These are "truly extraordinary." They are utterly unique in the market, and genuinely remarkable.
- This exercise will reveal whether a sufficient proportion of the projects are going to make a genuine difference.

EXERCISE: *Take a list of all existing projects. Scrutinize them by the three sets of criteria and place them in the relevant bucket. Look at the quantity in each. Review whether the balance is right. Use the findings to cancel unnecessary projects or search for more enterprising ones.*

BUSINESS IN

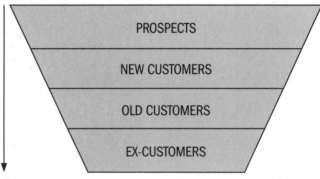

BUSINESS OUT

- This diagram can be viewed as a narrowing funnel, a tapering grain hopper or a plain old bucket.
- In most instances the wider top represents a larger volume or number.
- In this example, it is being used to look at the process of acquiring new customers.
- There are a large number of prospects who are not yet customers, and eventually a proportion become so.

- Over time new customers become old ones, and this increases the chances of them experiencing a problem with the product or service.
- If this dissatisfaction is not dealt with effectively, then they will leave and so become ex-customers.
- This sequence of 'business in' to 'business out' allows a company to analyse how many prospects are required to feed the business properly, and how customer satisfaction is working.
- If the volume of business leaving is too high in relation to that coming in, then it is a leaky bucket that needs urgent attention.

EXERCISE: Use the hopper to create a gradation from prospects to ex-customers. Populate each layer with numbers. Use the progression to work out whether the business is losing too many customers in relation to the new ones coming in. Put measures in place to rectify the discrepancy.

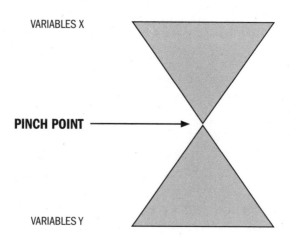

VARIABLES X

PINCH POINT ⟶

VARIABLES Y

- The Hour Glass is a highly flexible device that can be used conceptually or to demonstrate flow.
- In a conceptual context, it is often used to describe an entity that has plenty at the top and bottom, but very little in the middle.
- For example, that might be an organization that has plenty of senior management and lots of junior executives, but far fewer middle managers.

- This view can identify bottlenecks in workflow and approval procedures – as such, an hour glass business is most likely imbalanced and in need of attention.
- In a flow context, movement of materials or concepts can be viewed as starting broadly in a fair quantity at the top, whittling to a pinch point, and then expanding back outward at the base.
- An example might be considering 20 ideas, eliminating all but one of them, and then using that as a focus for everything that follows.

EXERCISE: *Use The Hour Glass to review a large quantity of options. Whittle to the winning idea. Then expand outward to look at all its possible manifestations. Consider adding a timeline to define when all the decisions will be made, and using it as a template to guide the next project.*

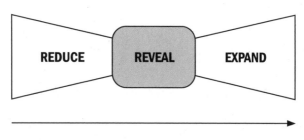

LINE OF ARGUMENT

- The Bow Tie is a horizontal cousin of the Hour Glass.
- It is a really simple depiction of how to tell an effective strategic story.
- The line of argument flows from left to right.
- Starting broadly on the left, many wide options and possibilities are considered and discussed.
- After investigation and analysis, these are gradually ruled out and reduced down.

- When the reduction of options is complete, the central idea, thought or theme is revealed.
- After pausing for a moment on the quality of what has been revealed, the idea is expanded out again to explain all its possible applications.
- This is the ideal way to tell a strategic story.

EXERCISE: *Choose a strategy or rationale that requires explaining in a presentation. Use The Bow Tie as a template. Start broad, explain how options were reduced down, reveal the central theme, and then expand on how it can be applied in many contexts.*

87

THE DECISION TREE

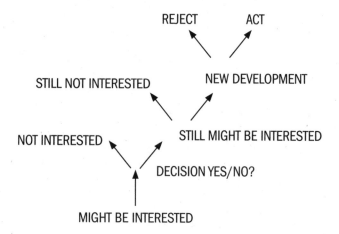

- The Decision Tree is a form of flow diagram that helps to map out complicated decision-making processes, or the possible directions a conversation or interaction might take.
- Each branch of a tree represents a decisive moment. This can be as clear cut as *yes/no*, or as mild as *not interested/might be*.

- The tree is particularly useful in mapping long and drawn-out sales decision processes such as buying a car, which might have a three-year gestation period.
- It can also be used to map options on questionnaires, the options in call centre conversations, or those on a technological interface such as a mobile device.
- More artistic representations can be generated using images of real trees, river tributaries, pathways, arteries and so on.

EXERCISE: *Choose a sales process that involves many small decisions – preferably a minimum of six steps. Plot the customer frame of mind from not interested all the way to a definite sale. Identify the defining decision moments and work out how to influence them in your favour.*

88

THE RIVERS AND DAMS CONCEPT

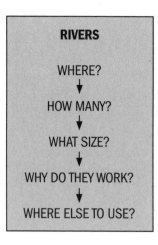

RIVERS

WHERE?
↓
HOW MANY?
↓
WHAT SIZE?
↓
WHY DO THEY WORK?
↓
WHERE ELSE TO USE?

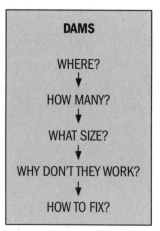

DAMS

WHERE?
↓
HOW MANY?
↓
WHAT SIZE?
↓
WHY DON'T THEY WORK?
↓
HOW TO FIX?

- The Rivers and Dams Concept looks at the flow of work in a company, and how well it functions.
- Rivers are things that work well. They run smoothly.
- Dams are blockages. They don't work well and they hold things up.
- In both cases, the first three questions are the same: where are they, how many are there, and what size are they?

- Since rivers are good, we then want to know why they work so well, and decide where else in the company we could use them.
- Since dams are bad, we need to know why they don't work, and work out how to fix them.
- If there is a large quantity of either to be dealt with, then the size question in each case enables a level of priority to be set on what to deal with first.

EXERCISE: *Choose a department, the whole company or a particular process that needs examination. Identify and categorize the rivers and dams. Run through the sequence of questions in each case. Now draw up a plan to increase the good things and fix the bad ones.*

OVER SERVICE
(DOING TOO MUCH)

SERVICE OVER
(NOT DOING ENOUGH)

- The Service Fulcrum examines the delicate balancing act between under- and over-delivery in service industries.
- The triangular fulcrum sits in the middle, and the horizontal line represents a well-balanced state of affairs – the correct amount of work being delivered to reflect the needs of the customer and the price being paid.
- If the service company does too much, they will be over servicing and thus eroding their margin – sometimes to the point of only breaking even, or even making a loss.

- If the service company does not do enough, it will be under-servicing and therefore failing to meet the needs of the customer. If this is the case, the service may well be 'over' because the customer might move the business.
- The diagram can be viewed alongside data (such as man hours, pricing and margin) to dramatize in what way the service level is imbalanced.

EXERCISE: *Choose a service relationship. Gather information about how it works, such as time spent, margin and profitability. See whether the company is over- or under-servicing. Take appropriate action.*

THE DEPERSONALIZING PROBLEMS CONCEPT

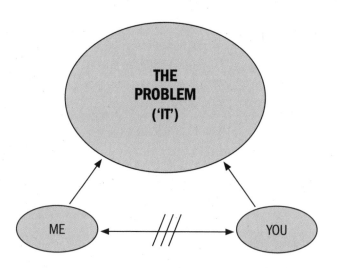

- The Depersonalizing Problems Concept helps to calm things down when everything has become too personal for comfort.
- Often in business, frustration with an aspect of work is centred on an individual rather than the issue. When this happens, language can become too personal.

- The horizontal line between 'me' and 'you' running across the bottom represents two people getting at each other, and the hashed vertical lines struck through it dramatize that language such as 'I', 'me' and 'you' don't work and should be avoided.
- Instead, the problem should be viewed as a large balloon, and should be described as 'it'.
- The plural 'we' should replace 'I', 'me' and 'you' when discussing the issue.
- Example phraseology might be: *"This is a serious problem isn't it? There are various different ways that we can use to solve it."*

EXERCISE: *Find an issue that has become too personal. Remove personal language from the discussion. Start looking at the problem as 'it'. Now propose solutions with the collective 'we'. Suggest the method to any colleagues who are getting at each other.*

91 THE ESSENTIALIST DIAGRAM

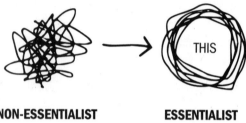

NON-ESSENTIALIST　　　　**ESSENTIALIST**

- Two diagrams in one. In his book *Essentialism*, Greg McKeown espouses the disciplined pursuit of less. The non-essentialist is all things to all people, pursues everything in an undisciplined way, and lives a life that does not satisfy.
- He or she thinks that almost everything is essential. It's the mess on the left.
- The essentialist does less but better, creating a life that really matters.
- He or she thinks that almost everything is non-essential, so if it isn't a clear yes, then it's a clear no. That's the clarity on the right.
- When it comes to energy, instead of doing many things half-heartedly, do one or two things properly. In both cases the same amount of energy is exerted.

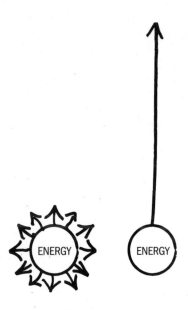

- It's the difference between a millimetre of progress in a million directions and significant progress in what matters most.

EXERCISE: *Look at your list of things to do. Go down it using an essentialist frame of mind. Cross out all the non-essential items. See what's left. Then go back through it again and ask yourself: "What is the one essential thing I need to do today?" Now do that, and that only. Repeat ad infinitum.*

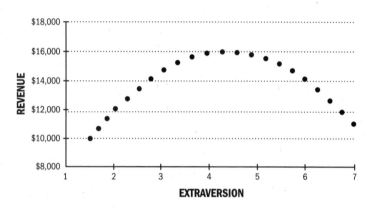

SALES REVENUE BY LEVELS OF EXTRAVERSION

SOURCE: ADAM GRANT, UNIVERSITY OF PENNSYLVANIA

- It's a commonly held belief that extraverts make the best salespeople, but a study by Adam Grant at the University of Pennsylvania blew all that apart.
- This Ambivert Arc shows the sales performance of introverts on the left through to extraverts on the right.

- Perhaps not surprisingly, extreme introverts have difficulty selling effectively. But so do extreme extraverts, usually because they show destructive behaviour, such as an excess of zeal and assertiveness, and a desire to contact customers too frequently.
- Those that succeed best are *ambiverts*. This is not a trendy new buzzword. It has been around since the 1920s, and is designed to describe those who can find the balance between being 'geared to inspect' and 'geared to respond.' It's a powerful combination, and hopefully of great interest to introverts the world over.

EXERCISE: *Start by regarding selling as simply persuading someone else that your point of view is valuable. Consider your next challenge of this type – a proposal or a presentation perhaps. Now balance the extremes of extraversion (too annoying) and introversion (too recessive). Pitch your stance accordingly with a blend of both.*

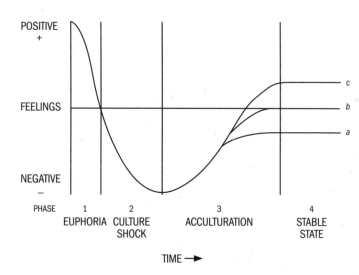

- The Acculturation Curve has all sorts of uses. The horizontal axis refers to feelings or mood state, with a positive/negative swing on the vertical axis. The suggestion is that most people acculturate through sharing and learning the traits and social patterns of a group.

- The curve will probably apply to anyone entering a new set up for the first time – moving to a new job, moving to a new country, students studying overseas and so on.
- Phase 1 is euphoria – a general excitement about the possibilities of the new situation. This is promptly followed by culture shock when it's all too bewildering. The acculturation takes place in phase 3, hopefully followed by a stable state in which the person is settled in their new environment. As with all models, this cannot be universally true but it is a helpful guide.
- The curve is in general use but the origin is usually traced to Hofstede & Hofstede who carried out so much important work on intercultural cooperation.

EXERCISE: *Consider your frame of mind and the conditions when entering a new situation (job, country, social group, etc.). Try to anticipate the stages your feelings may go through, and if possible attach a likely timeline to each phase. Alternatively, use the model to predict the behaviour of a new recruit or group of them.*

94 THE ELEVATE POSITIVES SALES STRATEGY

- This comes from Chip and Dan Heath's book *The Power Of Moments*. It's a huge revelation about where to put your sales effort. The customer experience research agency Forrester conducts an annual survey that asks 120,000 people to rate their customer experience from 1 (very bad) to 7 (very good).
- On average, companies spend 80% of their effort on Plan A – eliminating negatives by boosting customers on a score of 1-3 up to a 4, but this approach is not very effective.
- Plan B (elevating the 4-6s to a 7) creates nine times the value because the happiest people in any category spend more and there are dramatically more people in the feeling positive zone.

EXERCISE: Look at your sales and marketing effort. Where do you expend most of your effort? If the answer is a tendency to persuade those who aren't that interested in your product or service, or have mixed feelings about it, then investigate devoting more effort to those who are already (reasonably) well-disposed to you. It could reap better rewards.

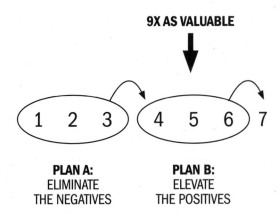

9X AS VALUABLE

1 2 3   4 5 6 7

PLAN A:
ELIMINATE
THE NEGATIVES

PLAN B:
ELEVATE
THE POSITIVES

- So-called T-shaped executives are highly valued because of their ability to show deep knowledge of a subject area and have the emotional intelligence to take a broad view across a whole company. The crossbar of the T demonstrates the breadth of their understanding of a business, and the vertical shows their deep specific knowledge.
- But in a modern multi-faceted business, a successful manager has to become adept on many fronts – a series of Ts in a row, with a profile more like a fine-toothed comb. This analogy was first raised by this author in *The Intelligent Work Book*.
- The moral of the story is that it doesn't work to only think big, or only concentrate on the detail. The successful modern senior executive needs to constantly be reviewing both big and small issues, zooming in and out regularly. Their expertise needs to span the fine-toothed comb.

EXERCISE: *If you aspire to being a successful senior executive, look at the entire range of what the company does. Do you understand and know enough about every area? If not, make it your business to find out enough about all of it. Only that way will you be able to find the right expertise in the organization precisely when you or a customer needs it.*

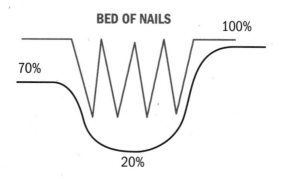

- Research shows that people remember 70% of the words at the beginning of a presentation, 20% in the middle, and 100% at the end. This applies whether the presentation is five minutes or an hour long. As a diagram, this pacing looks like a hammock.
- As a rough rule of thumb, all good presenters should grab their audience's attention immediately with something unexpected, show them an opportunity or something that threatens the business, identify the urgency of the problem, present a new way of looking at it, and demonstrate how their proposal will work.

- Beware the bed of nails in the middle where everyone gets bored. It should be your objective to get out of this phase as fast as possible.

EXERCISE: *Look at a presentation that you need to make. Review the hammock and the bed of nails shape in the diagram. Construct an arresting start and emphatic conclusion. Consider what case you need to build in the middle and keep the bed of nails as short as possible.*

OF DECISION MAKING

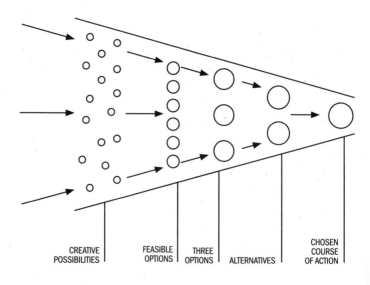

CREATIVE
POSSIBILITIES

FEASIBLE
OPTIONS

THREE
OPTIONS

ALTERNATIVES

CHOSEN
COURSE
OF ACTION

- The Lobster Pot Model of Decision Making appears in *The Art of Judgment* by John Adair. It is very similar in design to The Whittling Wedge in this book.
- A large number of creative possibilities enter the process on the left and are then subject to screening for feasibility. If they are impractical, they are rejected. As we proceed along the pot, we arrive at three options, reduce to two alternatives, and finally choose a course of action. It's a classic decision-making process – simple and clear.

EXERCISE: Choose a problem you are trying to solve, or a project that requires an inspired strategy or idea. Use any number of brainstorming techniques to generate a large number of possible ideas. Do not judge them too harshly at this stage. Then subject them all to a feasibility check: can they actually be implemented? Throw out those that cannot, and reduce the options down to three, then two. Then choose a winner.

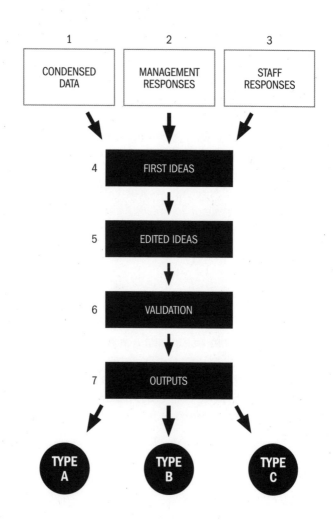

- The most important point when choosing the right method is to have one at all. No matter what you are working on, map out an initial sequence.
- In the example here, part one looks at all the available evidence. Part two examines the management view on the matter. Part three compares that with that of the staff. Part four outlines first ideas. They are then edited and validated, before being scrutinized for their most beneficial outputs.
- If you are struggling to generate a method, then select the most appropriate components you can think of and put them together in a logical order to reach a decision, ideally putting a time limit on each stage.

EXERCISE: *Choose a realistic number of stages based on the scale of the task, the degree of complexity and its importance. Sketch in what appear to be the most fruitful approaches, moving from explaining the challenge, to examining options, to generating new ideas, to whittling them to a manageable number, to a final decision, and suitable outputs.*

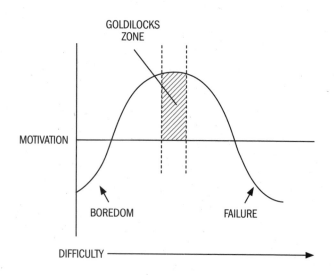

- The Goldilocks Rule has many manifestations. This particular diagram is from James Clear's *Atomic Habits*. It is a synthesis of a theory from psychological research known as the Yerkes-Dodson law, which describes the optimal level of arousal for decent motivation as somewhere between boredom and anxiety. It asserts that maximum motivation occurs when facing a challenge of just a manageable difficulty.

- In his classic book on how to achieve happiness, called *Flow*, the near-unpronounceable Drucker School of Management professor Mihaly Csikszentmihalyi was the first to articulate the concept of 'flow.' (His name is actually pronounced 'cheeks-sent-me-high,' and everyone calls him Mike apparently.) This is the state in which people are so involved in an activity that nothing else seems to matter.
- It usually involves a challenging activity that requires skills, the merging of action and awareness, and the paradox of control – there must be a sense of control, even if you are not quite sure how you are achieving it. This leads to a loss of self-consciousness and the transformation of time - hours can pass by in minutes, or minutes can stretch out to seem like hours.

EXERCISE: *Consider a task, possibly a new or somewhat daunting one. Examine how the flow works in relation to the diagram and see if you can tackle the task with a helpful attitude based on your understanding of how it is likely to work.*

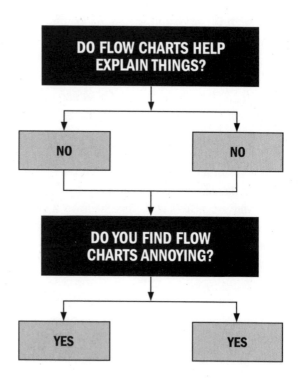

A piece of amusement to end with.

THE DON'T BE A
DICK FLOWCHART

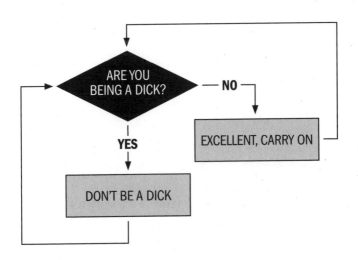

No explanation required here.

THE DIRECTION/
DESTINATION DILEMMA

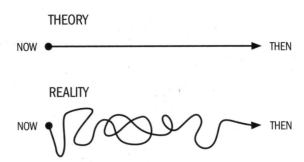

THEORY

NOW ●————————————————————————→ THEN

REALITY

NOW ●〰〰〰〰〰→ THEN

- Direction is a line or a course. It goes a certain way, but it's not the same as the destination.
- Barely any journey, whether physical or temporal, follows a single straight line. Most involve a number of directions, plural.
- This is particularly true in volatile categories where information is constantly changing.
- So your specific direction today may well be different from your direction tomorrow, even though the destination remains the same.
- Smart businesspeople understand that different directions are needed to reach the ultimate destination.
- This is additionally complex and distracting if the milestones you have set are so far in the future.
- Never forget your true destination, and don't confuse it with your direction today.

USEFUL DIAGRAMS BY TOPIC

Here are 25 common topics that people often have to deal with. Find the one that best describes what you are working on and then look at the relevant diagrams for inspiration. These are diagram numbers, not page numbers.

ACTION	19/40/51/59/72/73/78/91/97
COMMUNICATION	14/19/39/48/92/95/96
CONFLICT	11/19/24/31/56/58/86/90/93
CREATIVITY	12/13/25/30/44/57
CUSTOMERS	1/9/16/20/74/84/94
DATA	18/29/42/45/77/98
DECISIONS	18/19/32/34/55/72/73/78/87/97/98
EFFICIENCY	22/32/59/68/72/73/78/79/80/83/85/88/91/92/99
GROWTH	5/20/21/33/37/40/74/75/77/84
INNOVATION	12/13/15/28/74/75/77/83
LEADERSHIP	11/14/16/37/38/40/47/53/54/56/90/95
MOTIVATION	10/35/36/46/51/52/55/69/70/78/79/99
NEGOTIATION	7/24/26/31/38/57/76
ORGANIZATION	34/37/59/75/81/82
PLANNING	17/18/33/58/62/77/88
PRESENTING	3/4/5/15/50/76/86/96

APPENDIX 1
· · · · · · · · · · · · · · · · · ·

DIAGRAM SOURCES

All diagrams are originated by the author unless otherwise stated.

3. The Cone Of Learning: Edgar Dale 1969

11. The Five Dysfunctions Of A Team Pyramid: *The 5 Dysfunctions Of A Team*, Patrick Lencioni, (Jossey-Bass, 2002)

12. The Briefing Star: *The Ideas Book*, Kevin Duncan (LID, 2014)

14. The Trust and Cooperation Wedge: *The 7 Habits Of Highly Effective People*, Stephen Covey (Simon & Schuster, 1989)

16. The Inverted Leadership Pyramid: *No Bullshit Leadership*, Chris Hirst (Profile, 2019)

17. The Ishikawa Fishbone Diagram: *The Smart Solution Book*, David Cotton (Financial Times Publishing, 2016)

20. The Value Wedge: *Conversations That Win The Complex Sale*, Peterson & Riesterer (McGraw Hill 2011)

28. The Long Tail: *The Long Tail*, Chris Anderson (Random House, 2006)

30. The Gottschaldt Figurine: *Flicking Your Creative Switch*, Wayne Lotherington (John Wiley, 2003); *The Art Of Creative Thinking*, John Adair (Kogan Page, 1990)

31. The Win/Win Matrix: *The 7 Habits Of Highly Effective People*, Stephen Covey (Simon & Schuster, 1989)

32. The Time Management Matrix: *The 7 Habits Of Highly Effective People*, Stephen Covey (Simon & Schuster, 1989)

34. The Essential Intent Grid: *Essentialism*, Greg McKeown (Virgin 2014)

38. The Radical Candor Matrix: *Radical Candor*, Kim Scott (Pan Books, 2017)

51. The Resistance: *Linchpin*, Seth Godin (Piatkus, 2010)

52. The Ebbinghaus Illusion: *Left Brain Right Stuff*, Phil Rosenzweig (Profile, 2014)

53. The Golden Circle: *Start With Why*, Simon Sinek (Portfolio Penguin, 2009)

54. The Ideal Team Player Venn Diagram: *The Ideal Team Player*, Patrick Lencioni, (Jossey-Bass, 2016)

55. The #Now Diagram: *#Now*, Max McKeown (Aurum Press, 2016)

58. The Ethical Dilemma Grey Area: *Business Ethics*, Crane, Matten, Glozer & Spence (Oxford University Press, 2016)

59. The Indistractable Loop: *Indistractable*, Nir Eyal (Bloomsbury, 2020)

59. *Sleeping With Your Smart Phone*, Leslie Perlow (Harvard Business Review Press, 2012)

68. The Energy Line: *Making Ideas Happen*, Scott Belsky (Portfolio, 2010)

71. The Bar Code Day: *Sticky Wisdom*, Kingdon et al. (Capstone, 2002)

75. The Messy Middle Map: *The Messy Middle*, Scott Belsky (Portfolio Penguin, 2018)

76. The Rational Drowning Selling technique: *The Challenger Sale*, Dixon and Adamson (Portfolio Penguin, 2011)

77. The Innovation Shark's Fin: *Conversations That Win The Complex Sale*, Peterson & Riesterer (McGraw Hill 2011)

78. The 1% Better Every Day Curve: *Atomic Habits*, James Clear (Random House Business, 2018)

79. The Plateau Of Latent Potential: *Atomic Habits*, James Clear (Random House Business, 2018)

80. The Habit Line: *Atomic Habits*, James Clear
    (Random House Business, 2018)

83. The Three Buckets: *The Pirate Inside*, Adam Morgan (John Wiley, 2004)

91. The Essentialist Diagram: *Essentialism*, Greg McKeown (Virgin Books, 2014)

92. The Ambivert Arc: *To Sell Is Human*, Daniel Pink (Canongate, 2012)

93. The Acculturation Curve: *Cultures And Organizations*, Hofstede & Hofstede
    (McGraw Hill, 2005)

94. The Elevate Positives Sales Strategy: *The Power Of Moments*, Chip and
    Dan Heath (Bantam Press, 2017)

95. The Fine-Toothed Comb: *The Intelligent Work Book*, Kevin Duncan
    (LID, 2020)

97. The Lobster Pot Model of Decision Making: *The Art of Judgment* by
    John Adair (Bloomsbury Business, 2020)

99. The Goldilocks Rule: *Flow*, Mihaly Csikszentmihalyi (Rider, 2002)

APPENDIX 2

OVERSEAS EDITIONS

China	India	Poland
France	Italy	Romania
Germany	Japan	Spain
Greece	Korea	Sweden
Hungary	Netherlands	Thai

ABOUT THE AUTHOR

KEVIN DUNCAN is a business adviser, marketing expert, motivational speaker and author. After 20 years in advertising, he has spent the last 24 as an independent troubleshooter, advising companies on how to change their businesses for the better.

Contact the author for advice and training:
kevinduncanexpertadvice@gmail.com
expertadviceonline.com
thediagramsbook.com

Also by the author in the *Concise Advice* series:
The Bullshit-Free Book
The Business Bullshit Book
The Ideas Book
The Excellence Book
The Intelligent Work Book
The Smart Strategy Book
The Smart Thinking Book
The Sustainable Business Book

ISBN: 978-1-915951-07-6

ISBN: 978-1-911687-22-1

ISBN: 978-1-911687-53-5

ISBN: 978-1-911671-50-3

ISBN: 978-1-911687-94-8

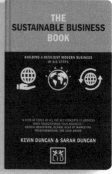

ISBN: 978-1-911687-40-5

ISBN: 978-1-911687-54-2

ISBN: 978-1-912555-70-3

ISBN: 978-1-911687-96-2